HILSEN FRA DANIELE, GREETINGS NORWAY

ALSO AVAILABLE BY DANIELE S. LONGO
Angels, Love, and Lost Souls: A Journey to Sicily

Hilsen fra Daniele, Greetings Norway

Daniele S. Longo

HILSEN FRA DANIELE, GREETINGS NORWAY
In Search of Purpose, Forgotten Friends, Northern Lights, and a Wallet.
Copyright © 2025 by Daniele S. Longo
All rights reserved
Published by Gerard and Sebastian, LLC

Inquiries should be addressed to Gerard and Sebastian, LLC
www.gerardandsebastiantravels.com
gerardandsebastiantravels@gmail.com
Shorewood, Minnesota
First Printing, November 2025

Library of Congress Control Number: 2025921689
ISBN 978-1-7376489-2-5 (Cloth)
ISBN 978-1-7376489-5-6 (Hardcover)
ISBN 978-1-7376489-4-9 (Paperback)
ISBN 978-1-7376489-3-2 (ebook)

Cover design by Daniele S. Longo
Cover photograph by Daniele S. Longo
Pictures by Daniele S. Longo
Itineraries: Maps edited with Canva. Photo overlays by the author.

All rights reserved. No part of this publication may be reproduced, stored in or reintroduced into a retrieval system, or transmitted, in any form, or by any means (e.g. electronic, photocopying, recording, or otherwise) whatsoever without written permission by the author and the above publisher of this book, except in the case of brief quotations embodied in critical articles and reviews.
Any use of this work to train generative artificial intelligence (AI) technologies to generate text/images is expressly prohibited. Your support for the author's rights is appreciated.

To my family, friends, and mentors.

Contents

Dedication	vii
Norway: A Car, A Map, and A Journey	xii
A Note from the Author	xiii
Prologue	xix

DAY 1	1
1 Sometimes, you need more than a Plan B	2
DAY 2	9
2 Cancellations, Delays, Tolls, and a Moose	10
- On the Road -	19
DAY 3	20
3 Norway, a Long (Exceptionally Long!) Country	21
- Nord Norge -	30
4 The Paris of the North	31
- Tromsø -	36
DAY 4	37
5 Restrooms, Senja Island, and the Pursuit of a Pen	38
- Senja Island -	47
6 Lofoten Islands: Scenery & Digital Payments	48
- Lofoten Islands -	56
DAY 5	57

7 Where Time Stands Still	58
- Namsskogan -	66
8 Just a Mess	67
- Driving South -	76
DAY 6	77
9 High on Hope	78
- Sognefjellet -	85
10 Uphill, Downhill, and Up Again	86
- Road to Flåm -	99
DAY 7	100
11 Reinunga	101
- From Reinungavatnet to Klevavatn -	109
DAY 8	110
12 På Gjensin Eden	111
- From Reinunga to Bergen -	121
DAY 9	122
13 Road to Hell(e)	123
- Hardangervidda -	131
14 Forgotten Friends and a Lost Wallet	132
- Friends (and Wallet), Here I Come! -	136
DAY 10	137
15 Frogner Park	138
- Frogner Park -	147
16 Rediscovering Downtown Oslo	148
- Oslo -	158
FULL CIRCLE	159
17 A Journey Ends, a New One Begins	160

EPILOGUE	162
Acknowledgements	164
Suggested Readings	166
Notes	167
About the Author	177

Norway: A Car, A Map, and A Journey

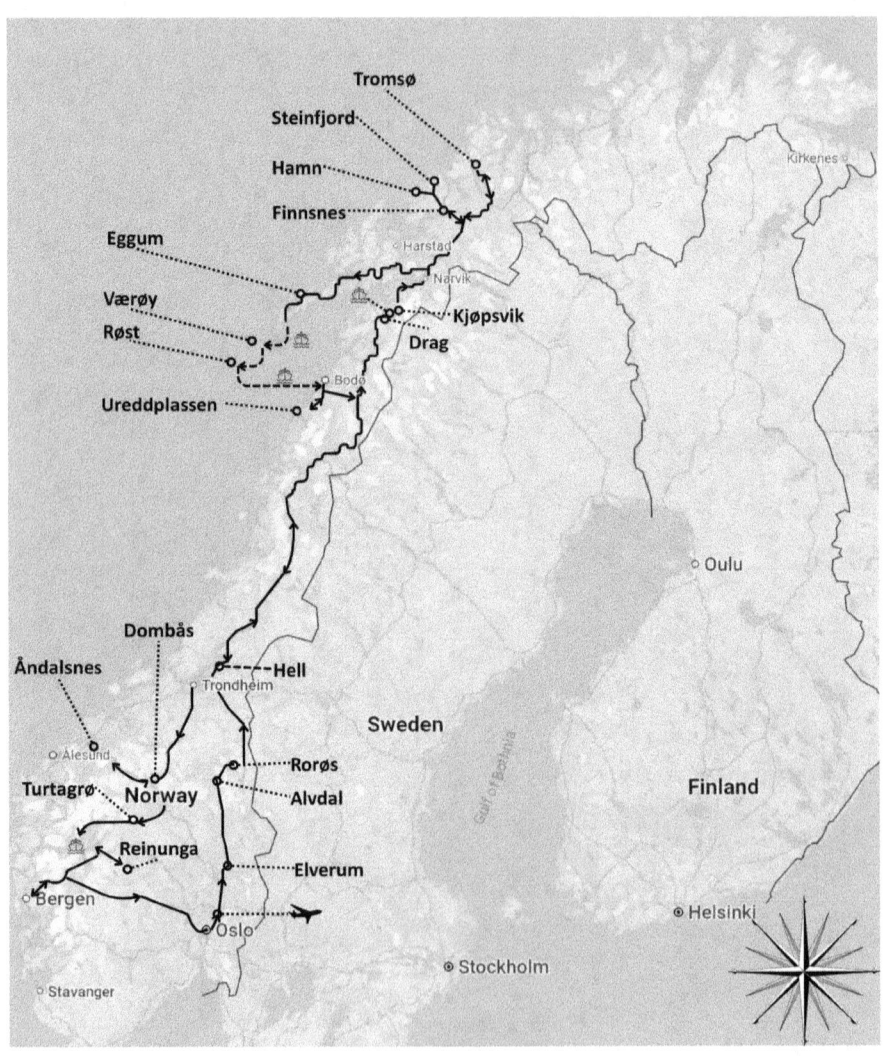

A Note from the Author

I WOULD HAVE PROBABLY SAT ON THIS BOOK'S TRAVEL NOTES, sketches and ideas had it not been for NaNoWriMo, National November Writing Month. The program gave me the opportunity to challenge myself to complete a first draft.

And I took it.

"Hilsen fra Daniele" started the emails I sent to four Norwegian friends I had not seen in person for more than two decades. Their intelligence, community engagement and passion for technology, history, and cultural preservation—not to mention their love for reading—have always been an inspiration to me.

For almost six years, I had the opportunity to spend my summers and most of my vacations in Norway. And during that time, as they shared with me their love for their country, they pushed me to better myself and learn new things. With them, I visited both large cities (e.g. Oslo, Trondheim, Stavanger, and Bergen) and smaller towns (e.g. Lillestrøm, Ryukan, and Årdalstangen), and I learned enough Norwegian to understand news headlines, and read the comic strips of Hägar Hardballene, *Hagar the Horrible*, and Helge, the moose.

Most of all, we hiked and explored. On my first trekking excursion to Vossevangen I blistered my untrained feet and slept in company of more sheep than humans. I thought I'd learned my lessons, and I physically prepared for my next mountain hike. I ditched my fancy Italian clothes and bought more comfortable and practical Norwegian attire. When I reached the top of Preikestolen, Pulpit Rock, at 604 meters (1,982 ft), my eyes soaked in the spellbinding views of Lysefjorden sending electrical signals of awe and wonder that permanently imprinted memories that filled my heart.

My calves though disagreed.

And that dichotomous feelings of amazement and pain lingered for days as I wobbled around like a drunk duck coming out of a pond.

And we ate.

Fish of all kinds, crabs, shrimps, game, berries were always at the table. May that *table* be a piece of furniture, a mountain rock, the seat of a boat, or the emerald green grass of a field—I also developed an addition to gjetost (goat brown cheese) layered on freshly baked bread and topped with berries.

After more than 2 decades since my last visit, I emailed my friends expressing my excitement for my upcoming trip to Norway and I asked if they would meet with me. Bjørn, Inger, Turil and Margit quickly replied with excitement.

* * *

I met Margit while studying Industrial Engineering at the Politecnico di Torino in Turin, Italy. At that time, I had joined a European student organization called B.E.S.T. (Board of European Students in Technology) and it was my responsibility to organize summer training courses for engineering student. Margit was one of the twenty students who attended one of the summer sessions. I admired her knowledge and participation in class, and most of all her ability to connect with all the other students on a personal level. Needless to say, when testing time came, her grade was one of the highest. After that summer course, Margit and I saw each other a few more times, in both Italy and Norway, and eventually our connection morphed into rare, few LinkedIn notes. When I asked Margit if she would be interested in meeting me for coffee or lunch during my trip to Norway, her positive reply came almost instantly. And when we met again at a coffee shop inside the train station it was like decades had not passed at all.

Margit shared with me the latest developments in engineering and architecture in Oslo, how the city had grown expanding in the Ocean's waters instead of depleting the woods, and how the city had started and grown to what it is today. She also shared many family stories from early life in the North of the country. What they would do in winter, what they would eat, how long it would take to travel from one place to another.

Bjørn is an industrial engineer. The first time I met him in Oslo, he owned a glue company. And as the main supplier of glue for the printing companies, he would always receive boxes of books created with his patented invention. His house had more books than its walls had wooden planks, and he would make it a point to read as many as he could. He was also a volunteer for Engineers without Borders, and I remember spending evenings mesmerized, listening to his stories of helping people in Mozambique, a country to which he would travel frequently to teach people how to use technology to better their lives.

Inger, Bjørn's wife, is the quintessential example of love and kindness. Inger was a teacher for children with special needs. For some reason, she made it her personal quest to help me learn Norwegian. For about four years, she would send me Norwegian books and packets of homework from Norway to Italy. I would fill out her paperwork and send it back to her. She would make corrections and then she would send me a new packet of assignments. Year after year, I'd like to think my Norwegian improved. I wish I could have kept up with my fluency. By the time I landed in Oslo in 2022, even though I had worked on practicing the language on Duolingo and Rosetta Stone, and I'd read books in Norwegian, my knowledge of the language was extremely poor. I could still understand, but when the time came to have a conversation, my tongue just could not articulate the right sounds.

I will never forget the first time we had dinner together together. At that time, I had a basic knowledge of English, and I didn't speak a word of Norwegian. I remember being very nervous and careful with every move I made. I wanted to make sure I made a good impression. I managed to have some decent conversation in broken English, and I like to think that my table manners were decent for most of the dinner time; until crab was served.

I had absolutely no idea what to do with a whole crustacean staring right to my face. I knew perfectly how to use knives and forks, as I had intensive training at the Naval Academy in Livorno during my Naval Officer training. But the Academy didn't teach me how to handle the tools needed to open and eat a crab. I quietly observed the other diners. When I felt comfortable, I grabbed the pinch and nipped at the crab. Nothing. Not even a scratch.

"You need to be more determined, Daniele," Inger told me.

I did. It was a disaster. The crab exploded in multiple pieces and parts of it landed graciously on the tablecloth and inside the other guests' plates and wine glasses. The tablecloth got stained all over—hopefully not permanently, but of course, she would never tell me.

"It happens all the time," smiled Inger. She stood up and got me another crab. This time, she showed me how to handle it. Still today, any time crab is served to me, I cringe.

While in Norway, I had lunch with Inger and Bjørn. I had forgotten how brilliant they are. The first time I met them, they showed me the design for their *retirement* home. It was a condo complex for them and their friends to live retirement years among the people they loved and with the comforts they would need as they aged. Twenty plus years later, when I parked my car at Bjørn and Inger's address, there it was. Not a design on paper, but the real building. They had managed to realize their dream. And the funny thing is that I knew where everything was. The design they had shown me two decades earlier was still in my mind. The only thing missing was the nurse's office. But Bjørn assured me that the office was not needed. Yet.

During lunch, Bjørn shared news about his latest engineering works in Italy, where he had purchased many old and semi-destroyed buildings and had returned them to life. Inger shared pictures of their hytta in Lillehammer and the pictures of her children and grandchildren. I had met her oldest grandchild many years ago. What once was a little infant was now a strong military leader!

The fourth person I wanted to meet again during my trip was Turil. Turil ignited in me the passion for Norway. During the almost six years I had the opportunity to visit her country, Turil showed me the beauty of her land–its diverse colors and landscapes, the fjords, the woods, the mountains, the beaches, and the waterfalls. Following her life journey, I discovered the friendliness and closeness of people living in both small villages and large cities. Most of all, I learned how to embrace and cultivate the Norwegian "Kos" state of mind: a way of living that values finding happiness and joy in the little things, being present and connected with the others, and basking in the gifts of nature.

* * *

This is a true account of my solo journey through Norway. Names and identifying characteristics of some individuals have been changed to protect their privacy.

Distances and milestones are reported in kilometers as Norway officially adopted the metric system in 1875. Maps of Norway and markers linked to specific locations and photos throughout the book are not true to scale.

The city of Ánslo, established in 1040 AD, was destroyed by fire in 1624 AD and subsequently renamed Christiania in honor of King Christian IV. The capital city of Norway became Kristiania in 1877, and finally Oslo in 1925. Throughout this book, the city's different names will be used according to their corresponding historical periods.

When planning a trip to Norway, be aware of seasonal conditions as mountain roads and local attractions may be closed. The weather is always unpredictable, wear clothes that can be layered. Regardless of the season, always bring a sweater with you!

Norway is a cashless society; be ready to pay with mobile apps.

Plan your visits to the local grocery stores in advance: most shops close by 6:00 p.m. during weekdays and may not open at all on Sundays. Wine is government-regulated and can only be purchased at Vinmonopolet stores.

Eat local. Try new things like Fårikål (lamb and cabbage), fiskesuppe (fish soup), brunost (caramelized brown cheese), crabs, herring, game (reindeer and elk), and krumkake. If anything, savor fish (e.g. cod, salmon), berries (try cloudbarries) and shrimps. On the road, load on baking goods such as rosinboller (raisin rolls), Wienerbrød (Danish pastries), skolebrød/skolboller (school buns made with cardamom dough and vanilla filling, sprinkled with coconut flakes), kanelboller (cinnamon buns), and waffles.

Most of all, explore, enjoy and let it go!

Prologue

I STARTED WRITING *Hilsen fra Daniele*[1], *Greetings Norway* on the fifth day of my journey across Norway, while hiking a scenic trail in Reinunga, a dream-like collection of *hytter* (cabins) that once accommodated local railway workers. Truth be told, I had recorded a few unstructured thoughts since I sat at the departure gate in the Minneapolis-St. Paul Airport, but the possibility of writing a book—sharing my excitement about hugging lost friends once more, my missteps and lessons learned, and even my uneasiness about traveling solo for the first time in twenty-plus years—did not come to me until I stopped racing from one place to another.

It was by the pristine waters of Lake Reinunga, at an altitude of 762 meters (2,500 feet) above sea level, that I really started to appreciate the physical and emotional journey I was going through. The crisp mountain air and the fall hues of the surrounding landscape were spellbinding. And even though it was impossible not to be riveted by the magnificence of the Flåm Valley, I had to remind myself that my trip would not last forever. As I stopped here and there, sitting by a waterfall or resting on a rock formation overlooking the lake, I started recalling places and scenes I had experienced in the previous days and recording some of my impressions. By the time I was on my way back to the hytta that had been my shelter for two days, I had a rough idea for format and content: *Hilsen fra Daniele, Greetings Norway* would be a novelistic travelogue to share the places and events I had experienced, but also to provide a feeling of what it was like to be a solo driver for 4,740 kilometers (about 3,000 miles) with limited time, a long list of places to see, and a car serving not only as transportation, but also as den, dining room, bedroom, and laundry room.

For the rest of the trip, I continued taking notes and pictures with the idea that I would, at some point, assemble them in an organized, meaningful way. I didn't want the book to be just a dry timeline of events embellished by photographs. I wanted to infuse it with the context and background that made my journey a transformative event—more than just a trip to a foreign country.

Many people reach a moment in life, as I had, when they feel something is missing—that they've lost that inner *spark* that drives them to achieve their dreams and motivates them to learn and grow each day. With this chronicle, I planned to share the way I reignited my creative fire and found myself again as I grappled with feelings of excitement and depression, happiness and anger, bliss and exhaustion.

It wasn't a perfect journey—I screwed up many times in barely ten days—but it worked, at least for me.

DAY 1

Excelsior, Minnesota

1

Sometimes, you need more than a Plan B

MINNEAPOLIS-SAINT PAUL INTERNATIONAL AIRPORT

I SIT AT THE GATE long before departure time for my first international solo trip in more than two decades and check my pockets over and over. These routine examinations of my few belongings would become obsessive for the next ten days. Yes, my passport and ID are still in the inside pocket of my jacket. Yes, my main wallet is securely zipped in the right pouch. And yes, my emergency cash wallet is set in place inside my left pocket[2].

Near me, a small piece of luggage and a backpack with a map of Norway sticking out of it. I'm not carrying much with me, as I want to be able to get in a rental car and start driving north as soon as I land. Checking a suitcase would require me to wait for it at Gardermoen Airport's baggage carousel in Oslo and waste valuable travel time. Furthermore, I don't want to take a chance to deal with lost or delayed luggage.

But there is another reason I'm traveling light. During my college years in Turin, Italy, I passionately crisscrossed Italy and Europe by car, train, and plane. Turin, a city bursting with history and vibrant culture, served as my launchpad for countless journeys. With rental cars, Eurail student pass cards, or University-sponsored flights, I ventured across the old continent, exploring everything from the historic castles of Poland and the majestic Alps to the sun-kissed coastlines of the French Riviera and the rugged Norwegian fjords.

After graduation, I continued to foster my insatiable curiosity and desire for exploration. While serving in the Italian Navy, I stopped by dozens of ports in Sicily and the Balearic Islands, and when my first corporate job opened the doors to the United Kingdom and France, I became the embodiment of a wanderlust-driven adventurer. I spent my scarce free time—and extremely limited savings—exploring London's magnificent museums and historical buildings, surfing in the freezing waters lapping Bamburgh Castle's sandy beach and driving to England's Lake District in my rusty second-hand car. In Edinburgh, Scotland, I found myself questioning the wisdom of my decision to attend the rugby match between England and Scotland as I stood outside the stadium. The air sizzled with tension as supporters of the English and Scottish teams marched uphill from opposite sides roaring in deafening choruses of chants and cheers; faces and body parts marked with old, ancestral symbols. The tragically introverted me thought I'd never make it back home alive.

In Paris, I spent hours savoring the collections of masterpieces housed inside the Louvre or taking sunset pictures of the Sacre Coeur de Montmartre. And when my life journey took me to United States for a three-month *temporary* assignment which lasted four years, I filled my weekends weaving my own American tapestry of friendships, cultural encounters, natural wonders, majestic cityscapes, and picturesque countryside settings.

But the once-familiar thrill of exploring new destinations and meeting strangers slowly faded as work deadlines, daily routines, and family obligations gradually filled my days. While I cherished the moments spent with loved ones and the long working hours I invested in building my professional career, I longed for the freedom and self-discovery that solo adventures had once offered and I patiently waited for the day when I could, once again, pack a backpack, set out on a new adventure, and reconnect with the explorer within.

This trip to Norway is a once-in-a-lifetime opportunity for me, at least for the time being, to travel solo with no timeline or lengthy list of reservations—just a list of places I want to see.

* * *

AS I WAIT FOR MY FLIGHT TO BE ANNOUNCED, I reflect on the events that brought me to Minneapolis-St. Paul International Airport. On a milestone birthday, my family asked what kind of present I wanted. Being at that stage in life when I don't really need any material thing, I asked for the gift of time. I just wanted some precious moments to do something special, like take a quick visit to a bookstore or a museum; maybe a few hours to drive up to Duluth and have lunch in Two Harbors.

"Why don't you take a full week?" my husband smiled. "Take a week for yourself and pursue something you'd like to do without the family."

I stared at him, speechless, trying to process whether he was joking with me. I must be honest; my husband has many qualities, but being funny is not one of them—and he loathes having to manage our hectic family schedule by himself.

"I am not joking," he said, looking straight into my eyes.

My brain quickly processed a few random options ranging from a scuba diving experience in the deep waters of the Virgin Islands, where a dear friend had just relocated, to a trip to the mountains of Machu Picchu, hiking on the Inca Trail. Even signing up for a week long archaeological experience or a yoga retreat made the list. As I evaluated the pros and cons of each option, I realized that there was something else I had wanted to do for a long time, and maybe this was the right time to do it.

The following week, I broke the news to my husband. It's our weekly Saturday routine to have some *couple time* at 318 Café in downtown Excelsior, Minnesota.

"I've decided what I am going to do with my gift of time," I started, as my husband dug into his avocado salmon toast.

"I am going to Norway to drive from Oslo to Tromsø and then find my way back to Oslo, driving through the Lofoten Islands, Trondheim, Trollstingen, Bergen, and Odda. No reservations or plans. Just me and a rental car for a week."

The color of his face quickly changed from rosy to pale. I didn't know if his physical reaction was linked to the salmon leaping down the wrong pipe, causing slow suffocation, or to my outlandish statement. "What did you say?" he finally asked, color slowly returning to his skin. "A solo road trip in a foreign country?"

"You do realize I was born in Italy, and the United States is already a foreign country to me, right?" I said.

"I know that, of course. But I mean, are you really planning to drive a car by yourself?"

"Yes, that is what *solo driving* means." I paused and quenched my sudden thirst with a glass of ice-cold water. "Don't worry, it's not a big issue. I know everything about Norway. It's going to be an easy, off-the-grid adventure." (At the time I made the statement, I had no idea how wrong I was as my journey would end up not being that easy at all.)

"Wait, off-the-grid? What do you mean with *off*?"

I wasn't sure how much sharing would be too much, but for some reason I didn't hold back. "I mean no plans or reservations, and sometimes no phone connection for about 4,000 kilometers[3]."

"Are you trying to scare me?"

"Of course not," I continued, looking straight to my breakfast plate as I knew I could not look at him in the eye. "You know, phone coverage can be spotty up on the mountains. I want to make sure you don't get too concerned if you can't reach out to me."

"Fine." Visibly frustrated, he went back to attacking his breakfast with an intensity that mirrored his inner agitation. His fork stabbed at the smoked salmon turning it into a chaotic disarray of pink flesh. Even the coffee wasn't spared; gulped down with complete disregard for the cost to his pharynx. Toast torn apart with ferocity, he stopped.

"I guess I'll have to deal with it."

"Thank you." I said, lightly patting his back. "Now I know I can count on you not freaking out while I'm gone—even when you won't be able to call me during my 8-hour boat ride between the Lofoten Islands and Bodø."

He suddenly froze, eyes staring at me with angst. I had shared too much. I wished I could take my words back, but it was too late. "Don't worry," I said trying to mitigate the situation. "I'm still working on the details, and I don't even have a date yet."

As it turned out, finding the right time was not easy. Even planning months in advance required me to find the perfect combination of time off from work, children's school and homework schedules for the kids, my husband's work commitments and COVID constraints. It seemed impossible, I must admit.

I thought I had found a good opportunity in the late summer of 2021. Work schedules seemed lighter, children were still on vacation, and soccer tournaments and cheerleading practices had not yet been set. But Norway kept its borders closed all through the fall, organizational changes made my work life more uncertain, kids' activities filled our calendars and COVID's Omicron strain hit the globe. My plans kept moving and moving.

Finally, in early fall of 2022 I found a window of opportunity and grabbed it. I knew it would be too late in the year to take advantage of long, sunny days, and that I may have had to deal with severe weather, but it was better than nothing. In case of sudden flight cancellations, I even set in place a plan B; I bought a one-way ticket from Amsterdam to Oslo on Norwegian Airlines. If my KLM/Delta flight from Amsterdam to Oslo were to be canceled or delayed, I could still hop on a different flight at the last minute.

At the beginning I really didn't want to plan anything. The idea was to just to get to Oslo's airport, rent a car and drive north all the way to Tromsø. From there, I would find my way back to Oslo, stopping here and there as needed. But the idea of having no scheduled rest time, and in the case of unreliable cellphone service, their being unable to call a hotel or B&B to check on me, did not pass my family's control-freak test. I had to make a handful of concessions, including making a couple of hotel reservations and creating a 50-page binder to document my entire itinerary. Details of the itinerary included specific information concerning the background of each key city or sightseeing spot where I planned to stop to take pictures, the approximate arrival time, and the length of my stay. The creation of the binder itself, with its itinerary and schedule, conflicted entirely with the overall purpose of an unscheduled, unplanned, and *leave-it-to-Mother Nature's-whims* type of journey, but I felt obliged to assure my family that I would make it safely back home. (Besides, I knew in my heart that my family members wouldn't read any of it anyway!)

Deciding what to bring with me and what to leave home should have been easy for someone like me, accustomed to managing projects, reimagining and automating work processes, and focusing on high-value, customer-facing transactions. It should have been a straightforward process of prioritization and elimination. But I underestimated a key external factor: my family. At first, I thought that a solo trip would be an experience concerning just one person—me. And my idealistic vision of myself truly needed little for the journey. But as I started packing, I realized that I had to accommodate a few heartfelt requests.

"Why don't you take a pair of nice pants?" asked my husband. "And maybe an elegant shirt as well, just in case you stop by a fine restaurant."

Of course, my children had to pitch in as well, reminding me that I would need fancy shoes. "And long socks, and thermal underwear," they added helpfully.

Further requests and *demands* for clothing items that I absolutely must include came from my friends in Cincinnati, and from my family in Italy as well. Finally, the Norwegian B&B host in Reinunga convinced me to bring a pair of waterproof boots for some obscure reason I could not understand at the time. My solo trip had officially morphed into a complex international affair.

* * *

SO HERE I AM, at the Minneapolis/St. Paul (MSP) airport, pacing up and down by the gate, waiting to leave for Amsterdam. The gate is crowded with passengers, and I can't stop wondering why they might be traveling to Amsterdam or to other, more distant destinations. Are they returning home after a trip to the United States? Are they traveling for business or pleasure? Are they longing to meet somebody in person after a long COVID-mandatory separation? Or maybe they are going to visit someone who needs their help. I could author countless stories based on my observations of what the travelers wear, the food they snack on, their behaviors, and even the nervous walks up-and-down the terminal hallways. And for all I know, somebody could be imagining a story while watching me, constantly checking my coat pockets, writing notes on a map, and waiting impatiently for my long-delayed birthday gift to begin. Once again, I review the exact location of my passport, wallet, backpack, and hand luggage.

I am ready.

DAY 2

A glimpse of Norway

2

Cancellations, Delays, Tolls, and a Moose

Thanks to the establishment of international time zones in 1883, I can travel in the *future* whenever I fly to Europe. By the time I reach cruising altitude, it's already midnight in Oslo[4]. I have about eight hours to settle in, check my itinerary, eat something, and most importantly sleep as much as I can: waiting for me in Oslo is a nearly 24-hour drive north before I can meet Njorun[5] in Tromsø and drift off in the cozy embrace of a real bed.

My seating arrangement is great; no passengers sit near me. I can fully cover my head with the hood of my warm, comfortable sweater and curl up in the space offered by a 21st century double seat in the main cabin—it's basically the equivalent of a 20th century full-size seat, as not everything is improving with the passage of time.

Lulled by the buzzing sound of the plane, I quickly fall asleep. All is well. For a few hours, at least.

* * *

HAVE YOU EVER EXPERIENCED that great feeling of waking up on a brand-new day, full of energy and plenty of options and opportunities? When I open my eyes, I'm ready to jump off the plane. In just five hours, I think, I'll be driving toward Hamar to take pictures of the medieval cathedral, stock the car with water and food, and find my way to Røros for photos, videos, and dinner at Restaurant 1897[6].

I put my jacket on top of the heavy sweater—I'm going to be too hot, but it's just temporary. Besides, by doing so, I have fewer items to carry with my hands. I check wallets and passports. My backpack is under the seat, and the small hand luggage is in the bin above me. I am ready to disembark.

As the plane lands in Amsterdam, that *everything-is-possible* feeling deflates like a helium balloon hit by a pin. My entire plan for a successful[7] Day 2 falls apart. A buzzing cellphone demands my attention now that cellular service is available. I check for any communication my family may have sent during my flight to Amsterdam. Dozens of messages quickly load...And there it is: a note from the airline company alerts me that my 8 a.m. connection has been canceled and my new flight to Oslo will now depart in the early afternoon. My first thought is to thank my instincts and pat myself on the back for having thought of plan B and purchased a ticket with a different airline company. Until another email, hidden between articles and ads, suddenly clouds my hopes: the flight with plan B airline got canceled as well and I have been rebooked on a flight landing in Oslo late in the evening. Even checking the large screens above the airport's transfer desk is useless; there are no other flights to Oslo. The best option to get to Norway at a decent time is to keep my original reservation and spend about eight hours of precious time in Amsterdam trying to keep myself from renting a car to drive from the world capital of tulips and perfume all the way north to Oslo.

To be honest, Schiphol[8], the main international airport in the Netherlands, is a wonderful place to be if you must spend a long time waiting for your next connection. You'll find stores of all kinds, gourmet restaurants, coffee shops and cocktail hangouts. If you need to unwind and reflect, you can spend time at the spa, stop by the meditation center, pick up a book at the airport library, peruse the Rijksmuseum's gallery space to visit several collections of Dutch paintings, or just stare at the *human* clock accurately tracking the time by tracing and deleting the clock's hands over and over. You won't even realize that the facility lies three meters (approximately ten feet) below sea level.

Although my trip was not supposed to be on a strict schedule, I'm still determined to reach Tromsø early in the afternoon of Day 3, and as I review my copy of the family binder, I recognize that I'll have to eliminate several stops from my wish list. Still resolved to accomplish a few milestones on my way to Røros, I stop by the Dutch Kitchen restaurant to drown my thoughts in syrupy waffles.

Eventually, the boarding call arrives, the gate opens, and passengers slowly shuffle onto the plane. Exhausted, but relieved that the wait is over, I settle into my seat. Just as I start to relax, the captain's voice crackles over the intercom informing us that we'll have to wait a little longer because a few suitcases are missing. A collective groan echoes through the cabin. Minutes tick by, slowly, until the last luggage has been located and loaded on the plane. When it seems we're about to take off, the captain delivers another disappointment: we've missed our takeoff window, and we must wait an additional thirty minutes for a new one. (During an earlier trip to Italy, just for fun, I created a *bingo* card replacing the usual numbers with all kinds of what-can-go-wrong possible scenarios. During that trip, I almost filled the card as flight delays, earthquakes, lava falls, ash clouds, rain, and fog impacted my trip. This Norwegian adventure is starting with a similar pattern.)

In the end, we leave Amsterdam for what is going to be a short hop to Norway. I look out the airplane window. Through gaps in a cloudy sky, I get a glimpse of Norway's green, luscious forests and deep blue waters. The snack onboard is just a simple sandwich, but I cherish that little treat as if I were dining at a Michelin 5-star restaurant. I've lost about five hours of travel time, and I can't afford any stops—not even for food or water.

* * *

I HAVE NEVER BEEN TO GARDEMOEN[9], Oslo's new international airport. The last time I was in Norway, more than two decades ago, Gardermoen was just a construction site. Today, the facility is impressive for both its modern architecture and its technology. And although it's almost forty minutes from Norway's capital city, its network of high speed and local rail transportation allows more than 70% of its passengers to commute using public transportation.

The airport is extremely straightforward to navigate, and I easily find the rental car agency I booked with. For some obscure reason I can only attribute to my overexcitement of finally making it to Norway or to my excessive caffeine intake, I decide to test my basic knowledge of Norwegian. I had been able to speak the language a little bit many years, jobs, and relocations ago. But without the opportunity to practice regularly, I have completely lost my skill. My attempt to have a simple conversation with the rental car team results in uproarious laughter. While Anders, the agent, processes my driving license, I ask where the closest cash machine is. "I'll need cash to pass through the toll gates." I explain.

"What toll gates?" Anders asks, puzzled.

The conversation is not going as well as I hoped. I quickly switch to English. "The ones on the freeway." I nervously start pairing my poorly articulated description of facts with Italian style body language and hand gestures, as if that'd make it up for my lack of knowledge of Norwegian language. "I need to add coins to the collection baskets to open the toll gate and proceed with my journey."

The agent looks at me as if I'm out of my mind. And I admit I would probably think the same. My eyes are bloodshot, my hair is a mess, and I've not had a shower since I left Minneapolis.

"We don't have baskets on the freeway, sir."

His colleague rescues him. "Well, we *did* have some kind of container to collect payments until the early 2000s. But nowadays, you just need to slow down, and a camera takes a picture of your car. We use your rental car deposit to pay the toll charges."

Having just dated myself from an entire generation, I apologize profusely and quickly sign any document I am given.

"Are you planning to drive in the city or on mountains?" asks the agent.

"This is Norway," I respond laughing. "Where would I go without driving on a mountain?"

The agent nods in agreement and hands me over the keys to a brand-new Volkswagen Passat Station Wagon. I had driven a similar vehicle as a younger driver in England. For the extravagant sum of 1,200 sterling pounds, I acquired a car almost as old as I was at that time, but still strong and reliable. Its roof may have released a few drops of water on rainy days, and its battery may have let me down sometimes, but as it was the first car I'd ever bought with my own money, to me it was as beautiful as a modern BMW. If the vehicle the agent gave me is going to be as reliable, sturdy, and powerful as my very first car, I've hit the jackpot.

I place the small luggage inside the truck of the car and snuggle my backpack on the passenger seat; seatbelt securely set in place and zips half open for easy access to snacks, water and my black binder. I grip the steering wheel. Smooth leather under my fingers, my solo road trip begins. I switch on the engine, ready for every twist and turn that awaits me.

The first stop is just minutes from Gardermoen airport itself. Gardermovegen is a road that leads from the airport to the small village of Sand and the royal burial mound of Raknehaugen[10], Rakne's Mound, Northern Europe's largest burial mound, built between 533 and 551 AD On my timetable, I am about five hours late. (Although I try to remind myself that I am not supposed to follow a scheduled plan at all, the sight of my thick, black binder pushes me to get going.) I pay my respects to the legendary King Rakne and move on through Innlandet[11], the only county in Norway without a coastline.

Formed in 2020 by the merger of the counties of Hedmark and Oppland, Innlandet covers almost one fifth of Norway's continental landmass and hosts Galdhøppiggen, the country's highest mountain, and Glomma, the longest river.

I drive through Minnesund, a small village set at the southern shore of Lake Mjøsa, the largest lake in Norway (and one of the deepest in Europe) and proceed north on European route E6, the two-lane (one lane each direction) main north-south road through Norway.

I'm just getting used to the car (and the pouring rain, which had begun half an hour earlier) when an obstacle I could add to my bingo card manifests: traffic congestion. As a result of the additional delay, I must skip a visit to Strandlykkja Church overlooking Lake Mjøsa and its scenic Ferrari red rest stop[12], the Viking settlement of Stange, and Hamar with its medieval cathedral. Even a quick stop at a REMA store (a no-frills grocery chain in Norway) is out of the question. I'll have to rely on the water bottle I received on the plane and the remaining snacks I carried inside my backpack to remain hydrated, and sugar powered.

The sun is setting when I reach Hamar: driving north to Lillehammer to take the scenic route to the Ringebu Stavkirke, Soholbergplassen, and Sollia Kirke would be impractical. Instead, I turn right at the crossing to cover as much ground as possible before dark on my way to Røros. The road sign points toward Elverum, home of Norway's Forest Museum[13] and entry point to the Glomma valley.

Travelers visiting Norway, are mostly fascinated by the country's dramatic coastal landscape, its glaciers, or other famous landmarks such as the Lofoten islands, and mostly overlook Norway's hidden gems. Located near the Swedish border, the Glomma, or Glåma, river is the longest and the most voluminous waterway in Norway. With a drainage basin that covers 13% of the entire country, the Glomma was Norway's main log-loading river and today generates enough hydroelectric power to provide energy for thousands of households. This silent travel companion will escort me on my quiet journey north until I'll reach Lake Aursunden, 130 kilometers (80 miles) southeast of Trondheim.

About 90 minutes north of Elverum, the rain stops, and in the darkness, a stark set of purple lights beams from the woods on my right to highlight the colossal structure of a silver elk guarding a rest stop. Atna's Storelgen[14], *Big Elk*, held the title of the tallest moose/elk sculpture from its construction in 2015 until 2019, when the Canadian "Mac the Moose" was gifted a larger set of antlers and regained its world title. I expected the metal body of Storelgen to be tall, and at 10 meters (32 feet), it is! Even in the middle of a dark night, Storelgen is massive. I quickly take a couple of pictures and clean up inside the simple rest facility. This is my first rest stop since the airport, and I'm still wearing my Minneapolis clothes.

I'm still about three hours behind schedule when I pass by Tynset, major producer of the "spark," kicksled, the Norwegian traditional form of transportation[15], and the few villages leading into the region of Trøndelag, the heart of Norway[16]. In the dark, I enter the old mining town of Røros.

Founded in mid-1600s, Røros owns its growth to the discovery of copper. Although the original settlement was destroyed by the Swedish troops in 1678 and 1679 during the Scanian war, the town was soon rebuilt. Today, Røros' church and more than eighty additional wooden buildings give the visitors a sense of what the town looked like in the early 1700s. Simple light fixtures cast a soft glow over the cobblestone street and the rainbow flags proudly displayed outside homes, stores, and public spaces. It's PRIDE week and couples of all kinds hold hands as they walk home. I take a walk to capture with my camera Røros' UNESCO-protected wooden homes and public buildings including the cathedral and Hyttklokka, the bell used to warn of fires and to mark the beginning and end of the miners' workday[17].

It's in Røros that for the first time I realize that driving an oversize Volkswagen Passat across Norway is not going to be ideal. Getting through its narrow, medieval streets is not an easy task. Stone walls weathered by centuries of history, harsh winters, and maybe other oversize cars, press close on either side. Ultimately, I identify a secure route to exit the town.

The city lights are fading behind me when a thick fog swallows the road ahead. For some reason, it feels entirely natural that I started my day stuck for hours in the crowded and cacophonic environment of Amsterdam's airport and now, as the final hour approaches, I drive on a lonely fog-bound road barely wide enough to handle two cars passing each other. The ground has been recently resurfaced and there is no signage indicating where cars are supposed to drive at an allowed speed of ninety kilometers per hour (approximately fifty-six miles per hour). The fact that I can barely see the narrow black ribbon swirling through a landscape that is completely hidden to me does not seem to concern the local drivers speeding to whatever destination awaits them.

But trying to avoid fast drivers on a pitch dark, foggy, unmarked road through the woods is just a small taste of what would be my first day driving experience in Norway at nighttime. The evening hours are the best time to learn about the local wildlife as foxes, cats and other creatures leisurely cross the road in front of me. All those afternoons spent playing Atari's "Out Run" on my way home from school in the 1980s were perfect training experience for skills I would need years later. Although during my *training* I don't recall having to deal with two bulky elk (one of which albino) sharing a little bit of quality time together, with no interest whatsoever in moving out of the middle of road until I pick up my camera to take a picture of them. Then they quickly disappear into the woods.

I pass through the mountain village of Glåmos, close to the Sakrisodden sanctuary of Norway's rarest plant, the Siberian Aster[18], and at lake Aursunden I pull over to the roadside and stop: I have reached the birthplace of the Glomma River, a whispering companion I have been traveling with since Elverum. I bid farewell to the waters that have guided me through the valley whispering secret stories of farms and hamlets as we passed through them together.

The real fun begins, I tell myself. I start the engine and move on. Rain, fog, cats, and foxes are my only companions as I drive through the mountain ski communities of Stugudalen, Ås, Selbu, and Elvran to reach my next destination: Hell.

Yes, Hell, Norway, is a real village; population about 1,600.

- On the Road -

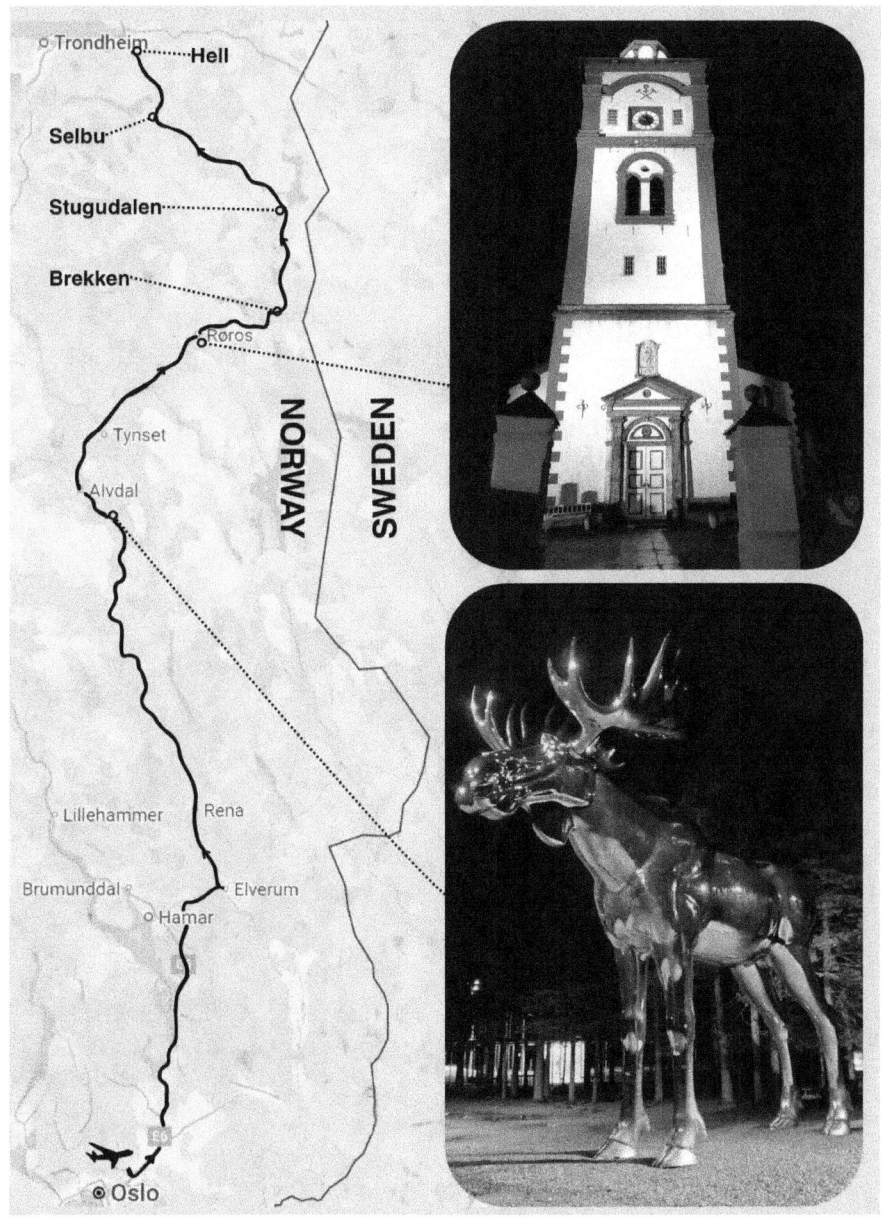

DAY 3

Saltfjellet

3

Norway, a Long (Exceptionally Long!) Country

IT'S COLD. Still, Hell is not frozen over[19] when I arrive at the outskirts of Hell[20], Trøndelag. I drive through the Hellbrua[21] bridge and wonder if I'm going to meet with some kind of modern Norwegian Charon[22] ferrying the souls of the departed through the Stjørdalselva River. But it's 1:30 a.m. and Charon must be sleeping like most human beings.

Both my car and I need a refill. I stop by a gas station just outside Trondheim's airport. All credit card machines have been disabled, and the station's front door is locked. Alone, the store manager protects his outpost: payments must be executed at a cash register window from which he sells hot dogs and water bottles to a lengthy line of customers looking for a satiating, warm, post-party, gas station fast food. After waiting in line for a while listening to the colorful exchanges between clients, mostly intoxicated, it's finally my turn to interact with the store manager. Johan, visibly tired but still friendly, shares with me the cost of a tankful of gas. And I wish I'd had some of those other customers' Saturday evening fun to balance off the shock of a bill above $100 USD—I jot down in my notebook a reminder to thank my rental car agent for giving me a hybrid!

I'm not sure if it's the smell of the hot dogs, the odor of the party goers or the reek of the gasoline—or maybe it's just me, in need of a shower—but I feel no desire for a late-night, hot dog. I just order a cup of coffee, dig into my last bar of dark chocolate, and move on toward Tromsø.

As I drive north, the road lighting grows dim and eventually disappears. It's dark and quiet except for a handful of trucks parked on the roadsides. It would be the perfect time for an encounter with one of Mother Nature's most spectacular sights, the Aurora Borealis. Every now and then, though I know that the thick blanket of clouds overhead is too dense, I scan the sky looking for the collision of sun-generated particles colliding with atoms of oxygen and nitrogen to create shimmering curtains sinuously opening portals to imaginary worlds.

With nothing but shadows to look at, I take the time to appreciate being alone on the road, with just music as a companion. After all, this is something I was looking for—an opportunity to be by myself and reflect on what's next, to evaluate new projects I could engage in (or stop doing), or to think about ways to help at home. Tapping my fingers on the steering wheel, I hum my way through quiet villages, turning this lonely stretch of road into my own music studio. My brain, however, is still in control mode. The radio becomes a code to decipher. It doesn't take long until I notice patterns in the sequence of songs, a repetitive cycle that becomes a sort of navigation system. I plot in the future how many miles I'll be able to cover until a new cycle of now-familiar tunes repeats. Glancing at the gas gauge, I forecast how many more song cycles I'll be listening to before the indicator demands a visit to a gas station, and I plan the efficient allocation of food and water to consume during scheduled breaks to ensure that supplies last until the next rest stop. The road ahead is unfamiliar to me and may be long and solitary, but in my mind, everything is under control and perfectly mapped out.

Around 4:45 a.m., I pass under Nordlandsporten, an archway so colorful it can't be missed, even in the darkest night. The gate's funky structure, inspired by the Aurora Borealis, marks the crossing point between Nord-Trøndelag and Nord-Norge, a place where the vastness of Norway can be felt.

Nord-Norge is a land of extremes ranging from the Lofoten Islands' obsidian peaks and Finnmark's glaciers, to Mo I Rana's Okstindan[23] high-mountain range, home of Oksskolten, the highest peak in Norway and Okstindbreen, one of the oldest glaciers. This region of striking islands, flat arctic elevations, and coastal forests encompasses 35% of Norway's landmass, but is home to less than 10% of Norway's population.

Driving through such an expanse of vast, scarcely populated land charges me with a blend of worry and excitement. The distance between Nordlandsporten and Finneidfjord, my next stop, is considerable, and I find myself constantly monitoring the gas gauge. Not all gas stations are open 24 hours a day, and I have more chances to cross paths with an elk than with another car. At the same time, as the headlights cut through the night illuminating only a narrow stretch of the empty road ahead, I try to push the rational side of my brain to embrace this feeling of vulnerability.

A few miles north of Mosjøen, dawn breaks over Lake Fustvatnet. The fog dissipates, revealing green forests blending into a teal blue background that gradually changes to lighter tones. It took me a while, but I start to feel the magic of Norway. Travelers visiting this corrugated, scenic and culturally diverse land experience its magic in different ways. For me, it's the feeling of being in a place lost in time, surrounded by the delightful sensory overload granted by dramatic landscapes, roaring waterfalls, fragrant woods, conversations with straightforward and caring people, and mouthwatering food. Not even persistent rain can take that feeling away. If anything, the combination of rain, fog, clouds, and spots of blue sky here and there adds more color and mystery.

When I reach Bjerka, 686 kilometers from Tromsø (426 miles), my delay has been reduced to less than one hour. I can start slowing down and enjoying my exploration of Nord-Norge. I pull over into a rest stop overlooking Vallabotnet, an inlet of the Ranfjorden fjord, to take a short walk on a pebble beach, breathe some fresh air and take in the views. Then it's time to follow the E6 zigzagging north, and I find myself singing the Backstreet Boys' "Tell Me Why" and Kim Carnes' "Bette Davis Eyes". I am in the vibe, as my kids would say.

I pass Mo I Rana to I enter Saltfjellet, one of the largest mountain ranges in Norway. The landscape suddenly changes, and the luscious green of the forest disappears into browns and strong reds until the trees give way to bare mountains and large areas covered by red moss and lichens. I've reached the Arctic Circle, the southernmost latitude where, on a summer day, the sun does not set. (But also, where on a winter day, twilight reigns.)

I have been longing to visit the Arctic region since I was a child. An avid reader of National Geographic magazines and biographies of famous explorers, the younger, introverted and shy version of me could never fathom that one day he would reach this part of the world.

I stop by the Arctic Circle Center[24] to walk over the marble path that marks the imaginary line of the Arctic Circle through the facility. Built in 1990, and set exactly at 66033', the Arctic Circle Center is a spaceship looking facility with a shop, a restaurant, restroom facilities and a movie theater.

"Funny, isn't it?" A young man points to the marble path I am walking on. "Excuse me?" I reply, puzzled.

"The path. It's supposed to mark the Arctic Circle."

"But it is. Isn't it?"

"Well, yes and no. The path still traces the imaginary line of latitude that marks the Arctic Circle on a map."

"But?" I ask, even though I know I should simply leave and enjoy the satisfaction of crossing something off my bucket list. Instead, I wait for an answer I may not want.

"The Earth's axial tilt changes constantly in a 40,000-year cycle shifting from an angle of 22.1 degrees to 24.5 degrees. As a result, the magnetic North Pole moves regularly and right now it's heading north about 14 to 15 meters per year (approximately 46 to 49 feet)."

"Interesting," my mouth sounds out, while my brain cries a word rhyming with *truck*.

"But do not worry," he goes on. "In about 44,000 years, the Arctic Circle will return exactly where you are standing right now."

"Good to know," I grin. "But if I didn't want to wait that long, where could I find the Arctic Circle today?"

"Let me check Google Maps." The man adjusts his glasses and checks his phone.

"Take your time," I say, mentally playing the Jeopardy! Tune.

"There it is!" He exclaims as if he just found the Holy Grail. "Go back on Saltfjellveien and drive north for about 2.3 kilometers[25]. Saltfjellveien crosses a mountain road. That's the current location of the Arctic Circle."

I thank him and quickly hit the road. Minutes later, I stop by the gravel path marking the present location of the Arctic Circle to capture some photographs.

Outside of my warm, metallic cocoon the temperature has dropped substantially. During my first trip to Norway, my friend Bjørn taught me everything I know about Norwegian culture and history. He also instructed me that "There is no such thing as harsh weather in Norway, just inefficient clothing[26]. The weather in Norway is cloudy by default. If it's sunny, go out and enjoy. It won't last long." During class, however, I must have missed details describing what makes clothes efficient. On that list, I would have probably found an essential item I did not bring with me: gloves. Something especially useful to have when you are roaming around in the Arctic Circle looking for the perfect photo shot. My fingers beg for the warmth of my heated steering wheel. But they can wait. All around me is a surreal combination of red rocks, tarnished-copper moss, and low vegetation. Snow caps the surrounding glaciered mountains, and here and there random purple flowers and aqua rocks add more alien touches. I may have compromised the health of my extremities, but I have fulfilled a childhood bucket list.

I continue driving north on the E6 on a valley carved by the Luonosjåhkå mountain stream. A few empty dwellings pepper the landscape and there are no vehicles or hikers in sight in any direction. I can't even imagine what life in the north of Norway must have been like prior to the construction of Saltfjellveien (Highway E6) in 1937, when the only way to reach Nord-Norge, about one third of the country, was by sea[27].

I think of sailors defying treacherous waters and rugged coastlines to bring supplies and news from the northern settlements, while I comfortably cruise my vessel entertained by Whitney Houston's "One Moment in Time" and Prince's acoustic virtuoso.

Flame-red trees suddenly border the road once again. A sign that I've been gradually driving downhill. At my next gas stop, I restock on rosinballer[28] buns, coffee and Kvikk Lunsj chocolate bars and then review my remaining route to Tromsø. Up to this moment, my logistic planning has been plagued by severe weather and uncertainty. Upon reaching the Saltdal Tourist Center, a rainbow comes out of the cloud. I take it as a good omen, trusting that things will change for the better.

* * *

I DRIVE TOWARD THE RAINBOW for about five miles. My spirits are high, the sun is shining, and the scenery is incredible. I attach my phone to the rear mirror and set it to auto mode, capturing pictures at scheduled intervals. This allows me to photograph landmarks like Kråkmotinden, a peak resembling black obsidian, without stopping.

I close to the next natural marvel on my list, Tysfjorden. With its 897-meter depth (about 2,900 feet.) below sea level, Tysfjorden is the deepest fjord in northern Norway and the home of the Homarus Gammarus[29], the world's northernmost variety of European lobster. Its exoskeleton is usually dark blue with white spots marking each crustacean's personal identity; a look quite different from typical heat-released pink of frozen product available in most grocery stores. This hard-shelled crustacean renowned for its delicious meat is so coveted by the locals that it's featured on Tysfjord's flag and coat of arms!

There are no roads, bridges or tunnels crossing Tysfjorden; the only way to reach the northern regions of Norway without driving through Sweden is to take a boat ride across the fjord. The original plan was to cross Tysfjorden at Bognes, but the pier has just been closed to allow for some engineering work. The $180 million, 10-year upgrade commitment[30], is part of an overall plan that will transform the entire Norwegian fleet from gasoline to electric power by 2024. Lucky me, Bognes is the first segment to be transformed. My only option is to drive south of Bognes and take a ferry at the port hamlet of Drag.

It's cold and windy when I reach the dock. I get in line with the few cars and trucks who will soon join me on my journey north. Tysfjorden's waters remain smooth enough to warrant a pleasant ferry crossing and soothe my anxiety about getting back on the road as soon as possible. I take the time to admire the majesty of the snowcapped surrounding mountains and the colors of the forests covering the island of Hulløya until my short boat ride ends at Kjøpsvik, or Gásluokta in Northern Sami language.

Kjøpsvik has a long history of mining and fish farming that can be discovered at the Kjøpsvik Museum, a non-profit, government sponsored organization that is part of Narvik's Museum Nord[31] network of historical institutions. The township is also the home for the majestic, obelisk-shaped Stetind, Norway's national mountain, and numerous other peaks and glaciers that separate this corrugated, narrow strip of of land from Sweden to the west.

About thirty minutes' drive north of Kjøpsvik, I get back on the E6 toward Tromsø. Three majestic suspension bridges cross the 1.7 kilometers-wide Efjord fjord (1.1 miles) and connect the two sides of the fjord to two small islands, opening the way to an expanse of woods that seems to go on forever. Or at least until the waters of Ofotfjord welcome me with a warm and affectionate embrace at Ballangen.

I have a special fondness for Ballangen. Many years ago, when I started reading books and articles about Scandinavian history and culture, I stumbled on a saga written by Snorri Sturluson, an Icelandic poet and historian[32]. In one of his works, the Heimskringla[33], *Orb of the World*, Snorri mentions Lodve Lange, which in Italian would translate "Lodve Longo". Lodve, born in Saltvik around 970 AD and first resident of Ballangen, was a Viking warrior who fought in the Battle of Svolder[34] on Olav[35] Tryggvason's longship Ormen Lange, Long Snake. During his reign, King Olav, had been able to unify the country after longstanding Danish attempts to control the region. But his achievement did not last long. At Svolder, King Olav Tryggvason's fleet was overwhelmed by a coalition led by Sweyn Forkbeard of Denmark and King Olav II of Sweden. After the battle, orphaned of its leader, Norway was once again split into provinces ruled by several leaders.

Nobody knows what happened to Lodve Lange after the battle. He may have died during the battle or was captured, spending the rest of his life longing for the time when Norway would be unified once again. What survived throughout history is Lodve Lange's love for his country and his willingness to sacrifice his life for it. The memorial erected by the E6 at Saltvik, between Ballangen and Narvik, is a testament of his significant role in Norwegian history. I will never know if I'm related to Lodve, but his life story is nevertheless inspiring.

About one hour north of Ballangen lies Narvik, a city both blessed and cursed by being the closest ice-free seaport to the Swedish iron ore fields of Kiruna and Gällivare. Its strategic location conferred Narvik key economic advantages, positioning the town as an essential hub for the transportation of iron ore, a cornerstone of industrial development in the early 20th century. But this strategic location made it also a coveted prize by both the Allies and the Axis Powers. The intense fighting that raged the city both by sea and land during WWII has been reported in many books and movies like "Narvik[36]", a 2022 historical film production.

I realize that my photo shooting affliction is worsening when I stop to join a group of seven photographers taking pictures of lake Øvre Sætervatnet and the surrounding mountains. We check each other's pictures and exchange ideas and tricks. I openly admit to not knowing how to capture perfect images, but they kindly help me figure out what I am doing wrong—which is basically everything.

- Nord Norge -

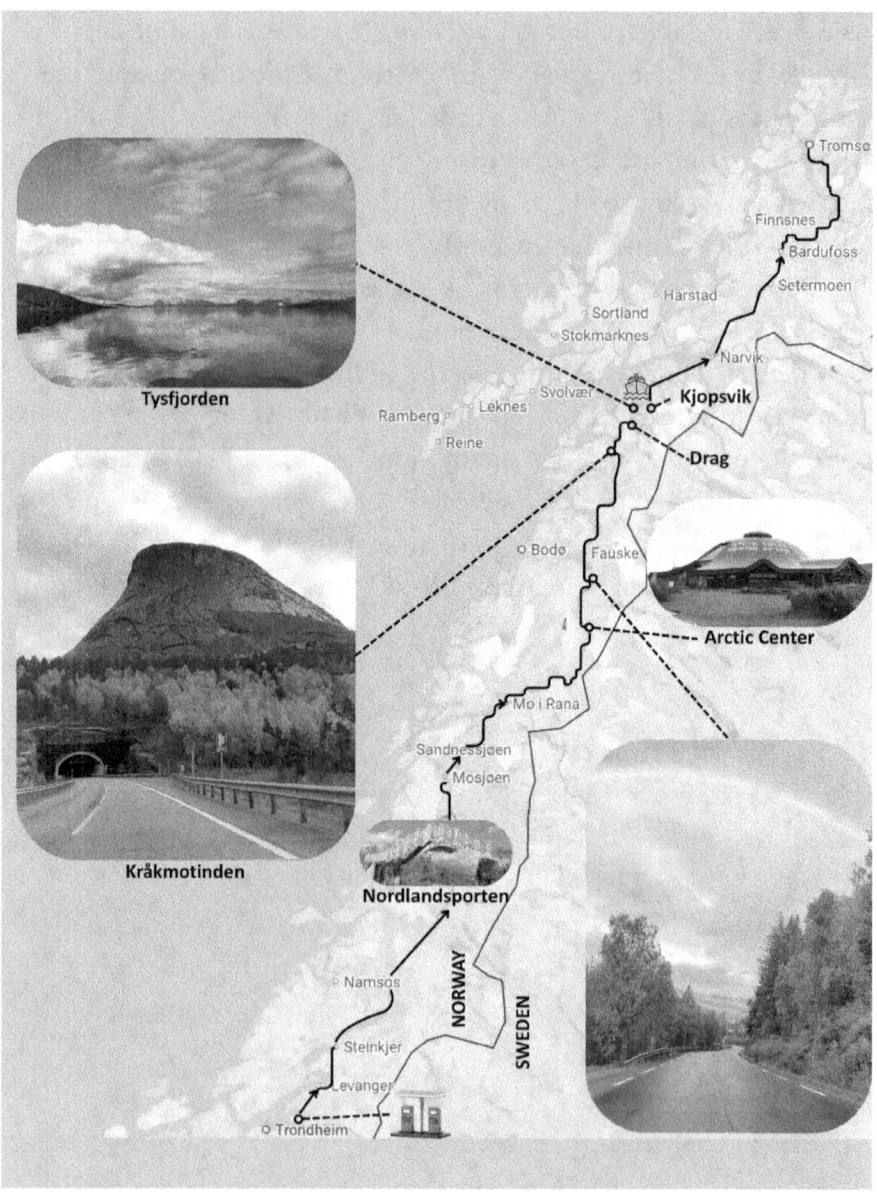

4

The Paris of the North

THE MILITARY SETTLEMENTS OF SETERMOEN[37] AND BARDUFOSS[38] are the last two cities I drive through before Tromsø. Both towns are small in size, but they represent significant hubs for military activities in the region. Here and there, a palpable military presence can be noticed, silently asserting itself against the spellbinding natural backdrop of never-ending forests. The sight of people in uniform and military vehicles stationed strategically along the route is a reminder of the strategic importance of this region to maintain peace and security not only for Norway, but for the Arctic region as well.

I reach the outskirts of Tromsø at about 5 p.m., just a few minutes behind my original schedule: I have only a few hours before sunset. My first stop is at the cable car to take pictures of Tromsø from the top of Storsteinen, *Big Rock*, a mountain ledge hovering over the city. I stop and ask for directions.

"The cable car is already closed, unfortunately. But you can hike with me up Storsteinen mountain," says a young man.

From the inside of my car, I stare at Gunnar, a tall bubbly man, full of energy and good spirit. Gunnar is planning to climb up the mountain and stop by his preferred sunset viewing spot. I have been driving for more than twenty-four hours, I haven't had a decent meal, a nap, or even a shower since I left the airport, and my lower half seems to have become one with the car. The idea of hiking the

Sherpatrappa[39], the 1,200-step path built by sherpas from Nepal, does not make the top of my list of things to do.

"Takk so mye, thank you," I kindly reply. And instead of joining my new friend Gunnar as he proudly makes his way uphill, I cross the Tromsø bridge and drive straight to the hotel. Set by Tromsø's marina, Hotel With[40] is charming: snow white wood, maritime feeling, polar accents, and perfectly located by the pier overlooking the western side of the city and the surrounding hills. The view of the marina and the bay is captivating, even from the top floor gym!

After a quick check-in, I leave my scarce belongings to the *fearsome* attention of a gigantic stuffed polar bear set by the front desk, and I drive the car to the nearby underground parking lot. Tromsø has a phenomenal parking infrastructure beneath most of the city center. As long as you can figure out a way to get inside the post apocalyptic style underground facility, you will find plenty of parking space. Tunnels and halls are lit with bright signage to indicate how many spots are still vacant and once again, having an oversize Passat wagon does not make life easy. Each narrow tunnel is filled with vehicles parked on both sides. My car's parking and collision warning sensors constantly beep as I attempt to squeeze my Passat into a maze of tight doorways opening to halls of parking spaces already occupied. Here I am, the guy who relies on technology to simplify life and guide me through the precarious task of parking, only to be overwhelmed by a symphony of aggravating warning signals harassing me as I play a game of automotive Tetris[41].

Aware of my tendency to get lost, I take multiple pictures of my car, my parking spot, and a few key directional signs and murals to help myself find the car tomorrow—I'm planning to leave early, and I have no intention of wasting time searching for my vehicle in the middle of the night.

Once out of the parking lot, I rush across the city to take as many pictures as possible before sunset. As the sun dips toward the horizon, one by one lights flicker on inside the wooden houses lining the narrow side streets. Tromsø's city center has the highest number of old wooden houses in northern Norway, some of them dating back to 1789, and in a perfect state of preservation. Nestled closely together along narrow streets, these homes create a cozy, welcoming atmosphere, their brightly colored exteriors standing in contrast to the rugged mountains and vast fjords surrounding the town. I wander around cobblestone streets, feeling like I am stepping into the pages of Cora Sandel's novels finding myself immersed in a world that once existed only in my mind, my own view of life in the northern region of Norway in early 1900s. I stop by small businesses expecting to meet Kvandal the tailor, Theodorsen the baker, or Dorum the goldsmith[42].

* * *

IT'S SATURDAY NIGHT, the streets are full of people, and loud crowds sing and shout by the marina where a live concert is being held. It's my first glimpse of the nightlife in the lively and energetic *Paris of the North.*

Tired and famished, I'm really looking forward to a nice meal. I've recently read that an infestation of king crab has caused the fisheries in the north to harvest more crabs than usual. In my mind, I have a clear vision of me sitting at an authentic Norwegian restaurant, cracking open legs and claws of a plump crustacean smothered in a butterbased blend of garlic, chives, and lemon juice. But when I ask around to locate the best seafood restaurant in town, I am repeatedly directed to Italian or American-style restaurants. What happened to all the Norwegian diners? My fish feast will have to take place somewhere else.

I may have given up on my ideal gourmet dinner, but I'm still hoping for some cinnamon-infused dessert. On Storgata, Tromsø's main pedestrian street, people of all ages and social status are having a fun time, and the restaurants, coffee shops, and street-food vendors have a steady stream of customers coming and going. I walk through a cacophonic ocean of languages and dialects from all over the world until I find a building displaying a "Delicatessen" sign. I enter quickly.

Inside the store, customers seem to be having fun, and the atmosphere is very lively—in fact, maybe *too* lively? I approach the counter and ask for a menu.

"Today we have a festival!" announces Agnetha, the charming baker whose nametag gleams in bold purple letters the baker, or the person I believe is the baker. Agnetha gives me a very colorful marketing piece and I'm already drooling in anticipation of tasting concoctions of sugar and spices made by prize-winning pastry chefs. But even the English menu is hard to decipher.

"Are these drinks, pastries, or appetizers?" I ask.

Puzzled, the *baker* stares at me. And I realize, maybe too late, that if a menu item is called "Cosmic Rainbow" or star-something unicorn, I've probably crashed a party not appropriate for a tired middle age solo-driver with a wake-up call set at 3:00 a.m. I kick myself for not picking up on it earlier and quickly leave the store, still craving sugar and cinnamon.

On my way to the hotel, I spot a more relaxed and subtle establishment where a gigantic espresso machine captures my attention. A few patrons sit at scattered tables, and I ask for a double shot of espresso—no pastries or cakes on the shelf. The barista tries several times to make a proper espresso. I am tired, and my social filter suddenly disintegrates.

"Kan jeg hjelpe deg? May I help you?" I offer, ready to volunteer to make my own coffee.

The barista looks at me, surprised. "Excuse me?"

"I am joking," I regain control. "You take your time. Just let me know when you are ready."

I find an empty table and open my notebook. While I await my longed-for coffee, I have plenty of time to record my daily adventures and look at the fascinating photos I've taken in the past 24 hours. I'm lost in my thoughts when the coffee arrives. Its bitterness hits me like a punch in the stomach.

"Is it good?" asks the barista.

I'm back to my Italian/Minnesota-nice state of mind. "Delicious!" I convincingly lie. I close my eyes, drink the remaining brown liquid in one gulp and then find my way back to the hotel.

A quick visit to the hotel's rooftop sauna followed by a long hot shower is a long due ritual for a body that needs a deep detox after a long drive. Warm steam and hot water have never felt so good.

- Tromsø -

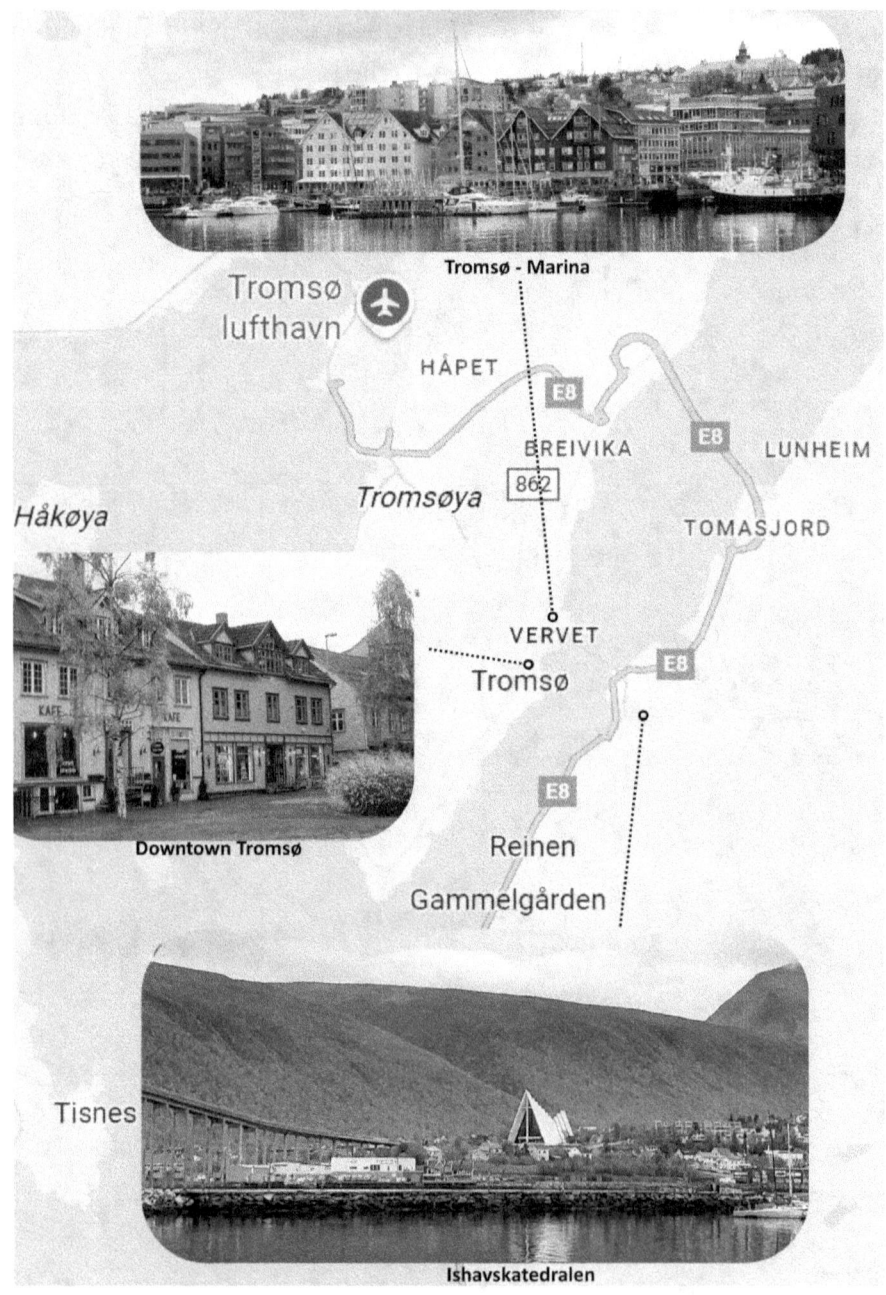

DAY 4

Steinfjord, Senja Island

5

Restrooms, Senja Island, and the Pursuit of a Pen

I WAKE UP AT 2:00 A.M. full of energy and excitement. The next couple of days are going to be exhilarating, but also extremely tiring. The clothes I washed in the shower last night (the same clothes I had worn since I left Minneapolis on Thursday afternoon) are still soaking wet. I put them in a plastic bag to be dried later inside the car (I'll hang them nicely on the back seats. Can't imagine what people looking at my car will think!)

On my way downstairs, I take a few interior shots of the polar exploration-themed Hotel With[43], including the polar bear set by the entrance door— an unofficial mascot, the night concierge tells me. I also take a selfie in front of a large mirror; I still look happy and cheerful, though I am a bit tired.

It's 3:00 a.m. and the city's nightlife is still in full swing when I leave the hotel. The air is thick with laughter, loud conversations, and the mingling scent of ethnic street food. Long lines of tired and hungry partygoers snake through the street, each leading to a different vendor, while a group of paramedics quietly monitor the situation from the sidelines.

Even though I had taken plenty of pictures to guide me back to the car the night before, I can't find my way to the underground parking lot. I approach a few people and ask for directions, but responses are a mix of confusion and good-natured attempts to help. One person points vaguely in a direction and struggles to remember street names, another one starts talking but gets distracted by her friends' parallel conversations. A loving couple, holding hands, starts laughing and admits they're just as lost as I am. The combination of the late hour and festive atmosphere renders the crowd a charming but ultimately unreliable source for direction.

Eventually, after a few unsuccessful attempts to gather information, I locate the statue that, according to one of my pictures, marks the entrance to the underground parking lot. Apparently, I had managed to pass the same spot multiple times without noticing the parking sign. I enter the gates to the underworld wondering with some amusement how I will make it back to Oslo when I can't even find my way to a parking garage.

Tromsø's bright city lights shine in the dark when I cross the Tromsø Bridge[44] to reach the mainland. The Ishavskatedralen[45], *Arctic Cathedral,* which is not a cathedral at all but a modern parish church of concrete and steel, welcomes me to the other side of the bridge. Its massive triangular facade marks my first milestone: I'm leaving behind the northernmost point of my journey. For the next two days, I have no hotel reservations, scheduled tourist visits or planned meetings. I just have to drive south and loosely find my way to Bodø.

It's a quiet drive in the dark with no locals, tourists, caravans or RVs on the road; which is great, as the road is quite narrow. Even when I pass by Mack Bryggeri, which used to be the world's northernmost brewery, my only travel companions are the radio and the occasional speed-trap machines I pass. As a curious engineer I've tried to understand these devices and failed miserably. Sometimes the green light is on top, sometimes at the bottom, Sometimes the camera has no lights at all. And I could swear I once saw a purple light (not a red one.)

Once again, I try to see the Northern lights. I stop here and there along Lavangsdalen Valley, switch off the car's lights, and in full darkness I look north. But luck is not on my side: no sight of nordlys[46] tonight.

* * *

THE SUN RISES OVER FINNSNES, gateway to the nearby island of Senja. The charming village of Finnsnes is overshadowed by the majestic shape of the Gisund Bridge, which connects the mainland to the village of Silsand on Senja Island. Although Senja Island is as spectacular as the more famous Lofoten archipelago, it's less traveled by tourists. Described as a miniature Norway[47] for its geographic mix that mirrors Norway's diverse landscape, Senja Island hosts a varied range of ecosystems ranging from its eastern, rolling grasslands to the steep mountains towering over the numerous fjords of its Atlantic coast.

The sound of "OMG" by Broiler and Sofiloud is pumping energy into the car, and I definitely need its vibrant, funky beat to awaken all my senses as fog slowly fills the landscape, massive elk leisurely cross in front of me, and occasional hikers randomly pop up on a road that rises and falls with a hypnotic tempo; its width too narrow to provide pedestrians with secure sidewalks.

When I reach Krokelvvatnet, the low, flat, grasslands give way to high mountains forming a barrier that years ago would have required people to travel by sea to get from one village to the other. Today, thanks to the Skaland tunnel the communities on the seashore can easily move in and out of their secluded inlets any time they want. But tourists do so, as well, and so again I pat myself on the back for not traveling during tourist season. The tunnel can barely afford one-way traffic, and a few waiting areas allow incoming vehicles to wait for a chance to get through in the other direction. After a few miles, I reach the first of my scheduled stops for the day: the Bergsbotn Utsiktsplattform. The panoramic viewpoint is just one of many attractions set on the Senja Island's Norwegian scenic route. The structure is shaped as a long, narrow sea wave platform leading to a dramatic view of the Bergsfjord inlet and its steep mountains dropping to the sea. The wave shape is not only magnificent, but also skillfully functional, as it allows people to take full-view pictures with the feeling of being suspended in air, which is a great sensation. (Well, unless the wind gusts get too strong.)

It's 6:30 a.m. in Norway (11:30 p.m. Central Time in the United States) when my daughter Valentina calls me. I'm taking pictures from the crest of the wave, holding my camera in one hand and a phone in the other. The strong wind hits me from my right side, and I can barely keep my balance on the platform. I should ignore the call, but then I remember that Valentina is attending a sleepover at one of her friends' homes—scenarios of all the things that could go wrong suddenly play inside my mind. I squat on the platform, trying to keep my balance while I answer the call.

"Hi papa," starts Valentina. Her voice is sad, and her tone is too low for such a spirited and energetic girl.

Oh no, oh no, what happened? screams my brain.

"How are you?" I answer instead, with a relaxed tone.

"I'm tired. I just wanted to check on you before I go to bed."

"Everything is going just fine, Valentina." My mood switches from worried to homesickness. "I wish you could be here with me to see how beautiful the view is." I set my camera's belt safely around my neck and stand up. "Let me put you on video call." I switch on the camera and show my daughter the view I am experiencing.

"Wow," she exclaims. "That is really beautiful!"

"Yes, indeed." I flip the camera back toward me. "Now, go to bed. It's late."

"Ok. Good night papa. I love you."

"Good night." My heart melts as I admire the view once again and turn back to the car. Time to get moving.

After a short drive downhill, I'm welcomed by the delightful village of Steinfjord, a small community of fewer than 30 people set at the shallow mouth of the fjord. The early morning light turns the half-moon shaped strip of land surrounding Steinfjord's pristine, sandy beach to copper and amber. To my right, the grasslands are already dotted with hikers on their way to the trail leading to Husfjellet, set at 635 meters above sea level.

Only a few miles away is another rest stop designed by the Transportation Authority. Tungeneset is a Siberian birch walkway leading to a rocky beach with a panoramic view of the North Sea and one of the island's most renowned and photographed landmarks, Mount Oksen, and its Okshornan[48] mountain range dramatically diving into the North Sea.

It's quiet down here by the shore. The fierce winds that battered Bergsbotn have no effect on this secluded promontory set between two fjords, as tall mountains frame and protect the landscape. A few seagulls scout for breakfast on top of granite rocks flattened by millennia of ice and water erosion. The scenery is spellbinding, and I try to imagine what life must have been just a few decades ago, when the tunnel beneath the mountains did not exist and this part of the island could be reached only by crossing icy waters in a boat.

Before heading east, I stop in Ersfjordstranda, a quaint fishing village on a beach so white and pristine that in a different climate zone it would be packed with tourists, beachgoers drinking Aperol spritz, and children building sandcastles. In the dim light of dawn on an early fall day, the beach is deserted except for a small tent, a few photographers setting up cameras by the shore, and me enjoying the scene from a perfect viewpoint near a gold-plated restroom by an empty parking lot. The clouds part, and behind me the rising sun makes its way between two craggy peaks. Its rays hit the restroom, lighting it up in gold, orange, and copper tones.

I try to freeze the moment with both camera and phone, but I can't find the right exposure or angle to capture this phenomenon correctly. Frustrated, I turn to the mountains, trying to seal the moment in my memory and possibly not burn my corneas. Eventually then face back to the restroom to take more pictures of the golden surface hit by the sunlight but the images I capture still don't look right. Each moment I grow angrier at myself for not having taken photography classes before the trip, and for not having purchased better equipment, or spending time with my friend Rob who knows everything about photography. And finally, in my futile frustration and repetitive attempts, I realize that I am missing this special moment that is happening in front of me. Right now! Soon the sun will be too bright, or it will move to a higher position, and this magic moment will disappear—and here I am, wasting time arguing with myself instead of enjoying it.

So, I stop. I turn to the mountains and the rising sun, close my eyes and feel the warmth of sunlight hitting my skin. And for just a moment, I feel like I, myself, I am glistening like the golden toilet. I do realize that sounds strange and kind of repelling, so I shall rephrase it: "I'm shining like the golden monument designed by Tupelo Arkitekture."

There you go. Now my description of overwhelming beauty sounds much better!

No matter how beautiful Ersfjordstranda is, I must drive back to Tungeneset, turn south to Straumsnes, and then east and uphill. I stop by the Bergsbotn Utsiktsplattform one last time. The rising sun is now splashing mountains and forests with warm light. Once again, no camera could possibly capture the beauty of this moment, so I leave that job to my memory.

At the crossing of Straumsbotn, I realize that I've spent too much time daydreaming and taking pictures. I'm late and I should move on toward the Lofoten islands, but instead of driving back to Finnsnes, I turn north, toward Hamn—because…why not? I'm already a bit late anyway. Besides, one of my *stretch* destinations is not far away, and even though I'll have to give up some break time later,

I feel that a trip to Senja would not be complete without visiting the Hamn lighthouse.

Hamn Harbor is a small fishing village on the northwestern coast of Senja Island, overlooking more than 90 islands dotting the Ocean. Although the setting faces the open waters of the Norwegian Sea, the homes, houseboats and hotels are protected by the fishhook shaped collection of small islands, breakwaters, and connecting bridges. There are only about ten residents in Hamn, but this quiet village, mostly converted to an idyllic fishing and photographic paradise, once supported the lives of more than 600 people, a nickel mine, one of the largest fish-trading posts in Norway, and the first hydroelectric power plant in Europe. Maybe one day I'll drive back with my friend Rick to fish for cod, halibut, or rose fish, and to spend time talking about the glories of the past with the few remaining residents.

On my way back to Finnsnes, I stop to take pictures of the Finnsæter Kirkegård, one of the most serene and panoramic graveyards I have ever seen. Its quiet and surreal setting must have had a completely different feeling just a few years earlier, when just on the other side of the street, the Senja Troll attracted thousands of visitors to the Troll park. Registered in the 1997 Guinness World Records as the largest troll in the world, Senja Troll stood 17.96 meters (58.9 ft) tall and weighed about 125,000 kilograms (138 tons). The colossal structure that made up Senjatrollet, his wife and their six offspring hosted a two-story adventure park until 2019, when it was destroyed by a fire.

I cross the Gisundet strait and leave behind me the rugged wilderness of Senja island. The 25-span Gisund Bridge stretching out for 1,147 meters (3,763 ft) ahead, guides me back to the more urban setting of Finnsnes, the administrative center of the Senja municipality.

From the height of the bridge, the view stretches wide. It's still early in the morning but sailing boats already speckle the sea like white pearls. The view brings to my mind a familiar scene. Any time I travel back home to Sicily, as the plane descends low over Catania, the sea below comes into focus peppered with white sailing boats and colorful fishing vessels swaying gently with the waves as friends and family members greet loved ones after a long journey.

After Finnsnes, I turn on the simpler (and narrower) road 855, instead of driving on country road 86, which would have been wider and faster, but longer route. It's still early in the morning, and traffic is scarce. I can venture out to lake Finnfjordvatnet and follow the Målselva River to Bardufoss.

It's in Bardufoss, population 2,500, that I experience once again, after many years away from Norway, the good hearts and helpfulness of the Norwegian people. This will also be the beginning of my love relationship with a chain of gas stations previously unfamiliar to me—Circle K. Its kind employees and unique operations will be a major help later in my trip.

For some reason, Bardufoss' small Heggelia Chapel captures my attention. The setting is perfect for a scene of a book I am writing about life in northern Norway in the early 1900s. I stop to take pictures and write a few notes.

Even though I had brought with me plenty of pens and pencils, none of my pens seems to work, and during the simplification and elimination process I used to pack for the trip, the idea of bringing with me a simple sharpening tool did not come to my mind. Determined to take notes at that very moment, and uncomfortable with using my own blood and a stick to accomplish the task, I stop by the nearby Circle K gas station. (I needed coffee, gas, chocolate, and rosinballer buns, anyway.) But to my surprise, there are no pencils or pens for sale at the gas station.

"I guess I'll have to take notes for my book on my phone," I tell the store manager.

"It won't be necessary," he replies. "Please, take mine."

"Are you sure?" I ask, surprised.

"Of course. Take my pen and write something nice about this region," he replies smiling.

I thank him and leave the store with a pen and a raisin roll so fragrant it fills my car (and my nostrils) with the smell of cardamom and butter. During my journey, I'd develop an addiction to these fluffy pastries stuffed with raisins, which I marry with a chunk of Kvikk Lunsj[49] chocolate bars. I know it may sound disgusting. But try it
once. You won't regret it, I promise.

As I fill my car with gas, I write a few notes to craft a scene of my novel. I imagine a couple coming out of Heggelia Chapel and stopping outside its door for a furtive kiss after having secretly gotten married. At that time, it seemed like the ideal setting for my book. A secret bond, sealed in 1919. Perfect.

Except that while researching the chapel's history a few hours later, during my boat ride to Bodø, I discover, to my disappointment, that the chapel did not exist until 1961. My story would need some "creative editing."

Fog and clouds finally give away to a clear, blue sky at Gratangen, just in time to allow me the rare chance to take an excellent shot of Gratangen Fjord before leaving the region of Troms og Finnmark and entering Nordland[50] at Bjerkvik, where I turn on the E10 looking forward to driving through the Lofoten Islands.

- Senja Island -

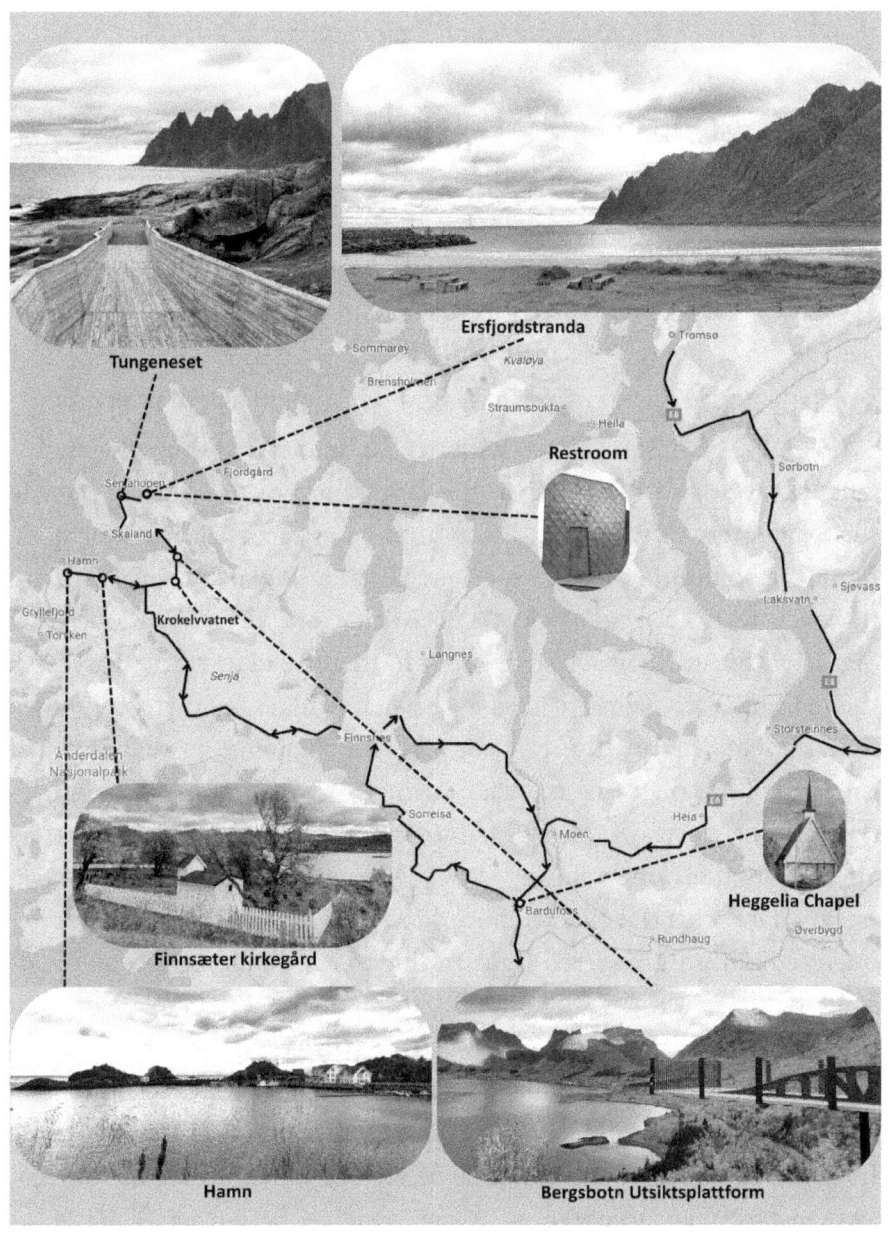

6

Lofoten Islands: Scenery & Digital Payments

THE TJELDSUND BRIDGE IS THE ENTRY POINT TO THE LOFOTEN ISLANDS, with its 32 spans that link the mainland to the island of Hinnøya, the largest island of Norway outside the Svalbard archipelago[51]. As soon as I start crossing the first span, I glimpse something I will experience over and over during my journey back to Oslo: roadwork! As in Minnesota, my U.S. adoptive[52] State, winter in Norway is extremely hard on road infrastructures. All the maintenance work needed by roads, bridges, and tunnels must be completed before the first snow. The challenge is that most of the roads I am planning to cross during my journey are already narrow, and if one way is under maintenance, what is left over is barely wide enough for one vehicle[53].

My date with the islands must wait for a few minutes, as I get acquainted with a green/red light traffic control system on the Tjeldsund Bridge. With no incoming cars and no personnel managing the flow of vehicles, I find myself trying to convince the apparatus to let me pass through. But the device is incorruptible, resolute, and stone deaf to my supplications. So, I try a more creative approach; I switch off the car. In the blink of an eye, the traffic control light switches from red to green.

Shaped like an arm branching out to the open sea, Lofoten is an archipelago of a dozen significant islands and hundreds of smaller islets and rocks. Most of the larger islands are linked by bridges or tunnels except for Røst and Værøy, which can be reached only by boat. About a million visitors cross the Tjeldsund Bridge every year, attracted by the stunning beauty of the islands, the majestic peaks dramatically jutting out of the ocean, the sandy beaches sheltering emerald green pastures and secluded coves, and the open oceans hiding the world's largest known deep-water coral reef[54]. But if you are a Sicilian food lover like me, the Lofoten Islands represent the legendary ancestral home of stockfish, or as we say in Sicily, Stoccafisso[55]. The relationship between Sicily and stockfish dates to the Norman presence on the island and southern Italy between 999 AD and 1250 AD, and I am on a quest to find the drying flakes[56] on which the fish is cured for about three months before being moved to an indoor facility. There the process of preservation will continue for two additional months. The best Norwegian stockfish comes from the islands of Værøy and Røst, which are only accessible by boat. And I'm bound and determined to set my eyes on their shores.

Once I cross the Tjeldsund Bridge, the E10 gently follows the curves of Hinnøya's shoreline and passes through sheltered beaches, secluded bays, and small villages set against the backdrop of towering mountains. Seen from above, Hinnøya, Split Island, looks like the two gigantic wings of a butterfly basking in the sunshine, its antennae tickled by the northern waters of Gullesfjorden, and its abdomen lulled by the southern waves of Kanstadfjorden.

Harstad, set on the green lowlands of the northern edge of the butterfly's eastern wing, is the only large city on the island; a few farms, small villages and the Møysalen National Park sprinkle the remaining rough and mountainous land. West of Hinnøya, connected by the Raftsund Bridge, is Austvågøya. Heaven for mountain climbers, Austvågøya is an island of mountains so steep that many areas, like the world-renowned Trollfjord, can be reached only by sea.

There is no shortage of beauty in Austvågøya, and on such a sunny day a new perfect shot awaits at each turn and twist of the E10. The sky is so clear that from the sandy beaches of Myrland, the distant peaks of the outer islands seem easily within reach, although a boat ride from Austvågøya to Hadseløya, its closest neighbor, would take more than 40 minutes. It's already 1:45 p.m. when I reach the Austnesfjorden Rasteplass, another welldesigned picnic area set on a majestic viewpoint to allow tourists to walk about and capture stunning pictures of the surrounding landscape.

The Austnesfjorden rest stop, like others in Norway, was created with the aim of protecting the natural environment. Its floating walkways shield the local ecosystem from being destroyed by crowds of tourists that visit the islands and indiscriminately walk on moss, grass, and flower beds. By channeling the directional flow of visitors, the walkways preserve the beauty of the landscape for everyone. The rest stop is the perfect viewpoint from which to take pictures of the Austnes Fjord, the countryside and the Sildpollnes Chapel, a church set on a peninsula in the middle of the fjord and surrounded by mighty peaks.

I'm starting to get tired and hungry, but I still have a long way to go and not much time left. My meander through the hills and beaches of Austvågøya to take pictures and videos has burned up my chance to take a break for a gourmet meal[57].

As I drive through Svolvær, I dream of a 5-star fish dinner experienced inside a genuine, top-rated restaurant setting with real forks, knives, and table setting. Instead, the only thing I can do is open the rooftop to fill the car with salt water-infused fresh air and snack on rosinboller buns, Kvikk Lunsj chocolate, and lukewarm coffee I purchased earlier that morning in Finnsnes. By the time my lunch is over, I'm on the Gimsøystraumen Bridge between Austvågøya and the small island of Gimsøya[58], a great place to enjoy the view of the midnight sun in summer.

The Sundklakkstraumen Bridge links Gimsøya to Vestvågøya, the original Lofoten Island,[59] home to the Torvdalshalsen rest area[60], Eggum, and an extensive list of construction zones. But the time spent waiting at traffic control lights and the delays caused by reduced-speed driving on narrow lanes is totally worth it.

Torvdalshalsen Rasteplass is a picnic area designed with benches and tables for visitors to relax, rest and enjoy the views of Vestvågøya Island. And if the weather is nice and sunny, it's a pleasant place to replenish vitamin D deficiency or walk up and down to take pictures and loosen up stiff legs that are tired of being jammed in a car. As I reach the outskirts of Bøstad, in the central part of the island of Vestvågøya, I make a poor choice. Fooled by the feeling that I caught up with my schedule and I have plenty of time to spare before my ferry ride to Bodø, I turn north to visit the Eggum Rasteplass instead of staying on the E-10. Even though my rational brain warns me that I'm making a mistake, my heart takes over.

As soon as I leave the two-lane E10, I enter the one-lane (for both directions) Hovdveien toward Eggum. The narrow width of the road and the slow traffic gives me a hint that the 15-minute journey estimated by my navigation system will easily last twice as long. But I'm still under the magic spell of the islands, and with the rooftop open to a blue sky, instead of listening to my gut instinct, I lip-sync the Norwegian pop music playing on my radio. Not even the 10-minute wait for an oncoming car to pass through a bridge too narrow for two cars bothers me.

When I reach Kvalhausen, a hill north of Eggum used as a radar station by German forces during WWI, and today transformed to a rest area, my Nirvana state-of-mind suddenly implodes like the popovers I try (unsuccessfully) to make every holiday season. The weather changes for the worse, the temperature drops, and the restroom facilities I desperately need to use are closed for the season. Tired and hungry, I check the time. I'm late. Maybe too late.

The final 80 kilometers (about 40 miles) between Eggum and Moskenes are a chaotic combination of roadwork, slow drivers, detours to even narrower (if that's even possible) roads and a series of woolen barriers of fluffy, sluggish sheep that have no intention of letting me pass. The lack of clear signage marking directions to the ferry makes the drive even more exciting.

Trying to avoid some of the construction zones, I get lost in the process a few times. It's just thanks to a very nice resident of the beautiful village of Reine that I barely manage to reach the docks in Moskenes before the ferry to Bodø leaves. I stop the car by the parking lot to step out of the car and turn to the Moskenes' church set high on the hilltops.

"Thank you." I say a little prayer.

In the parking lot, it's just one RV and me.

"Are you going to Bodø?" I ask the driver in my imperfect Norwegian. "I think that the boat in front of us is the one we need to take," I suggest—as if I were an expert in travels across Norway.

"Yes, we are going to Bodø," replies his wife. "But the next boat won't leave until tomorrow."

Puzzled, I wonder if I misunderstood the statement or if I really missed my ride to the mainland.

"Hi." Hans, a representative of the Moskenes-to-Bodø ferry approaches.

"Is this the ferry to Bodø?" I ask.

"Yes, it is." Hans answers. "We leave in a few minutes. But this boat will stop in Værøy and Røst, as well. We'll be in Bodø in about eight hours. Sometime around 12 a.m."

I turn to my neighbors sitting inside the RV. The couple looks tired. The man, slouched in the driver's seat, stares out the windshield toward somewhere out in the seat. The woman sitting at the passenger seat looks similarly weary. "Why don't you take this boat?" I ask her.

"The trip is too long and circuitous." Dark circles shadow her eyes reflecting the weight of their travels. "We'll wait for the boat that leaves at 12 a.m. The trip will only take four hours and we'll be in Bodø by 4 a.m."

No reason to debate about why they would prefer to spend the entire evening waiting in a parking lot when they could instead enjoy the ride to two additional Lofoten Islands and still dock in Bodø earlier than the next boat. I nod offering a sympathetic smile and I wish her good luck.

"Are you going to board?" Hans' calm, deep voice interjects.

"Of course," I answer, looking forward to resting for a few hours and maybe eating something that resembles a real meal. "Here is my card," I say, presenting my credit card as a form of payment.

"We don't accept credit cards or cash."

"How can I pay, then?" I ask, confused.

The answer "We only take mobile payments or online bookings," should have been expected by someone like me, who works daily with technology and artificial intelligence. But in the context of my unplanned, free-spirit and solo-driving journey, it did not click right away.

"I don't have any mobile payment option. Is there anything you could do to help me?" I ask. A poor reply, I know. It only takes a few moments playing with a phone and a couple of apps to set up mobile payments. Had I taken the time to set up the mobile (e.g., Wallet, PayPal, Apple Pay, or the Norwegian app Vipps) on the spot, I would have saved myself a lot of trouble just a few hours later.

Norway is one of the most cashless societies in the world. Most transactions are executed via mobile wallets. And sometimes, there is no human interaction involved at all in the execution of a financial transaction. For instance, as I drove north from Oslo to Tromsø, cameras set on top of toll stations took a photo of my license plate and charged the rental car company directly.

"Park the car[61] inside the ferry," Hans says, smiling. "There is a cash register on the second floor by the restaurant. I'll join you upstairs to notify the teller that you will pay for the transfer using your credit card."

I thank him and park in my assigned spot, between the starboard of the boat and a large truck. Sending another prayer to Moskenes' church, I wish for a calm sail across the Norwegian Sea to avoid any opportunity for the truck to disengage itself from the safety equipment and hit my car.

By the time I get to the restaurant, the ferry has already left Moskenes. I'm still thinking about the missed opportunity of a gourmet fish lunch in Svolvær, but the closest thing to a *seafood spectacular* I can buy on the ferry is a shrimp sandwich. It's still a great upgrade from my usual meal of raisin buns, chocolate, and coffee.

When time comes to pay for my meal, I ask the cashier to add to the bill the cost of the transfer to Bodø.

"Excuse me?" she replies in English.

Confident that miscommunication is due to my broken Norwegian, I repeat, in English, what the ferry attendant had told me to do.

"What do you mean?" The cashier looks at me like if *I've smoked my socks*[62]. "You should have paid the fee at time of boarding!"

As my mind starts processing all kinds of scenarios, including a rush of angry mobs shouting at me as the ferry turns around to return to Moskenes, or the release of my car (with me inside) to the welcoming embrace of Vestfjorden's deep waters, the cashier calls her manager and Hans for a quick meeting in the kitchen area. I must confess that I've never seen any Norwegian arguing, but based on my observation of the exchange of assertive words shared, I can certainly state that I have caused quite a bit of trouble for Hans. In the end, the manager allows me to pay at the cash register with my credit card and everything goes back to business as usual—which, for me was to take as many pictures as possible before sunset.

It's pitch dark when we dock at Røstlandet on the island of Røst, and I wish I could see beyond the buildings around the pier. In the darkness, I imagine to be in the same spot where, in 1432 AD, an Italian ship was hit by a storm on its way to Flanders[63] and the survivors of its wreckage stranded on a small island near Røst. One of the survivors, Captain Pietro Querini, described life on the island, including what the inhabitants traded, farmed and, most of all, ate. It is attributed to Pietro Querini the introduction of stockfish in Italian cuisine and as the boat leaves Røstlandet, I can't stop thinking about my mother's family Stockfish recipe.

It would be a perfect opportunity for an encounter with the Northern lights, but the weather does not cooperate: a storm approaches and thick clouds cover the sky. As passengers deal with sea sickness, I thank my 18 months of experience in the Navy, when I spent weeks at sea on a 60-person boat. I find a comfortable lounge chair and fall asleep, lulled by the gentle waves.

- Lofoten Islands -

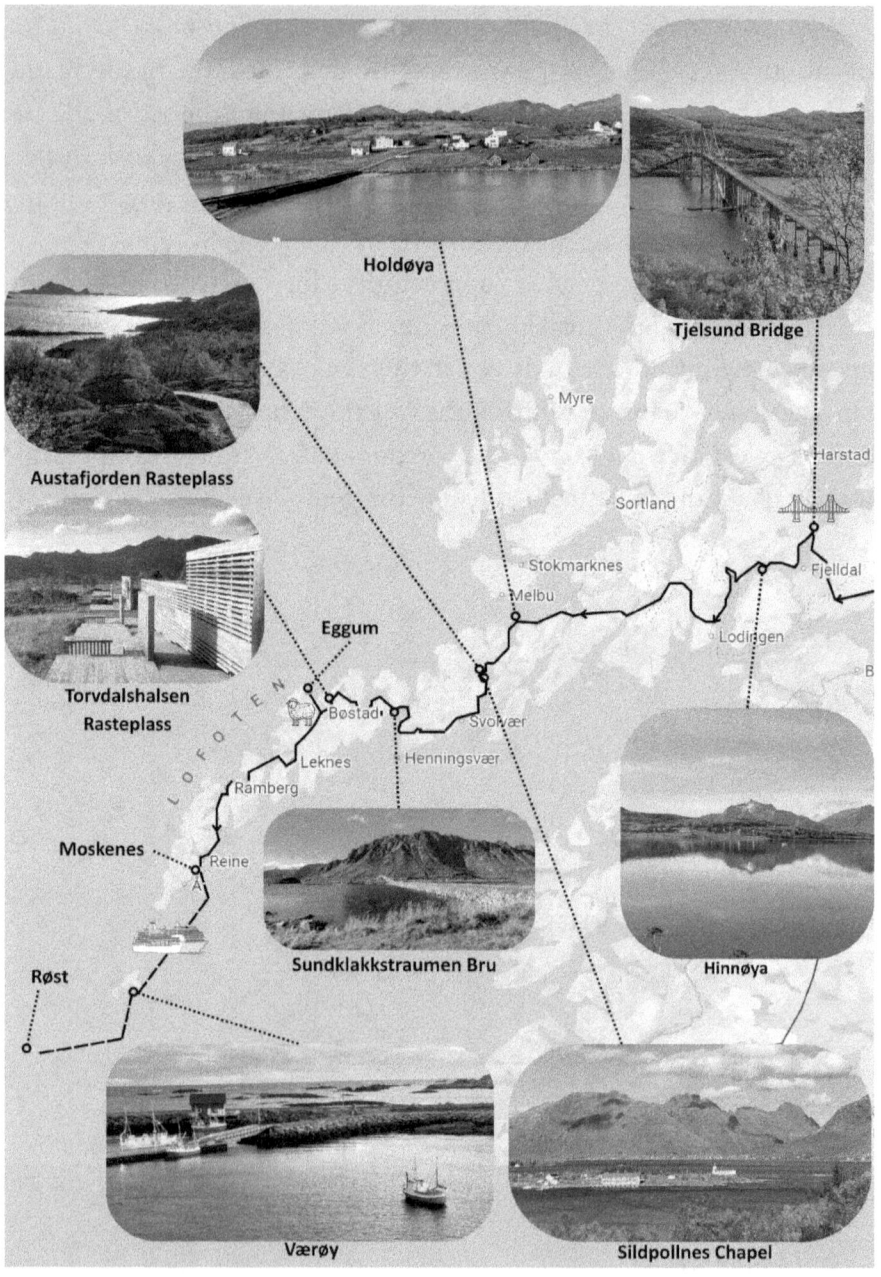

DAY 5

Gartland, Norway

7

Where Time Stands Still

AT ABOUT MIDNIGHT, THE FERRY DOCKS IN BODØ. I've had a few hours of sleep, donned a fresh set of clothes and, thanks to the amenities available on board (large, clean restrooms), I don't smell like a sheep grazing on top of the Sicilian hills of Mount Etna in the middle of August. I feel good and energized, and I'm ready for the next leg of my trip: Ureddplassen.

Defined as one of "the most beautiful public restroom in Norway,"[64] Ureddplassen is a wave-shape bathroom facility with a viewing terrace overlooking the open Norwegian Sea. The realization of such a touristic attraction did not come cheap[65] and on a dark night like this, it would be the perfect place for a view of the northern lights.

My plan for the day is already quite intense, as I need to drive about 1,100 km (approximately 684 miles) south to reach Åndalsnes. But as I have plenty of nighttime hours to drive and enthusiastic energy to spare, the idea of adding a deviation of 1.5 hours each way to my plan does not seem that demanding.

It's the only shot I have, my brain, drunk on adrenaline, tells the rest of my body. *How challenging can that be?* I cross the Tverlandsbrua Bridge and follow my heart as I pass Løding and turn left on the FV17.

On my way to Ureddplassen, I traverse the bridge of Saltstraumen, a small village set on a strait characterized by one of the strongest tidal currents in the world.

Four times a day, 400 million cubic meters of seawater flow in and out Saltfjorden and Skjerstadfjorden, generating loud and impressive whirlpools[66]. When I cross the Saltstraumen bridge, the road is completely deserted, dark and quiet. The next tidal event won't happen for a few hours and there are no tourists taking pictures of the whirlpools, but inside my car, it's a different story. Harry Styles is singing "As it Was" at the top of his lungs, and I rhythmically hum and join the lyrics here and there, in a once-in-a-lifetime Styles-Longo private concert on wheels.

It's about 1:45 a.m. when approximately 5 kilometers (3 miles) from Ureddplassen, a road worker stops me at the entrance of a tunnel. To my dismay, I find out that the tunnel I need to pass through to reach the rest stop will remain closed for maintenance work until 5:30 a.m. I still have 760 kilometers (472 miles) waiting for me to reach Trondheim, and from there, an additional 300 kilometers (4.5 Google hours) to get to my next stop in Åndalsnes. It breaks my heart, but I have no time to waste. Now I must drive all the way back to Løding (1.5 hours) to catch up with my original itinerary. *I could have slept for three hours in Bodø!*

The only positive spin I have is the hope for good weather and a possible encounter with the northern lights. While driving north back to Løding, I see something up in the sky and I stop in a remote parking lot. With me, there is just another photographer scouting the firmament with a very elaborate and expensive apparatus. I switch off the lights of my car and approach him.

"Have you seen anything tonight?" I ask.

The photographer disengages from the camera "You just missed them." He slowly starts packing his equipment. "But you may be lucky. If you drive north, toward Bodø, you may be able to catch them."

I thank him and move on. The more I drive north, the more frustrated I get: no northern lights in sight. At some point, I stop in an empty parking lot in the middle of nowhere and switch off the car.

I get out of the vehicle keeping a hold on its metallic frame. Woods surround me completely, and for the first time in my life I can see, feel, smell, and hear...nothing. Not a bit of light piercing the cloudy sky, nor the sound of birds chirping from their nests. Not even the sound of leaves moving gently in the wind. Nothing.

In complete blackness, I wait and wait for my night vision to kick in until the sudden rattle of my car startles me, reminding me that standing alone in the dark, in a remote location, in the middle of the night, is probably not a great idea. I get back inside the car, lock the doors and start the engine; it's time to move on once again.

There are no other vehicles in sight. The lack of slow drivers is just one of the many perks of driving at night: truck drivers are a rarity, waiting times in the proximity of roadwork areas are shorter (or at least that's how it feels), and very few distractions avert your attention. With that said, you still must look out for animals in the road, as elk, foxes, sheep, and some kind of very large lemur or possum love roaming around at night.

It's at Fauske that I regain a sense of time and place. After hours of navigating in the dark, driving through the center of the "Marble Capital[67]" of Norway feels like driving through Times Square in New York City with its brightly lit streets and business signs. But that feeling is short-lived. As soon as I leave Fauske, it's dark once again.

I'm driving south, tracing the same path I took on my way up to Tromsø. The only difference is that my journey, this time, is not as scenic as before. The blue waters of Saltdal's fjord, Rognan's historically poignant crossing leading to Blodkorset and the Blodveimuseet[68], the powerful currents of the Luonosjahka River, everything is shrouded in obscurity—even Ørfjellet's peak and the moss and lichens surrounding the Arctic Center.

It is dawn when I stop by the city of Mo in the county of Rana, or simply Mo I Rana[69] for a quick gas purchase, a warm rosinboller bun and some caffeine intake. The third largest city in Nord-Norge, after Tromsø and Bodø, Mo I Rana[70] is rich in natural resources, industries, and cultural diversity. To Havmann, Man of the Sea, I send a silent greeting with the promise to return to Mo I Rana for a longer time and properly appreciate the uniqueness of its sturdy granite outline emerging from the sea. As the sun rises over valleys and mountains that two days earlier were cloaked under clouds and fog on my way to Tromsø, its rays brush the landscape with a kaleidoscopic explosion of colors in all shades of greens, browns, yellows and reds that melt into blue waters of the surrounding lakes and streams. It's going to be a great day for pictures and videos.

My recent caffeine rush lasts only about two hours. A few miles north of Trofors I find a quiet, panoramic rest stop surrounded by thick woods, and I can't think of a better place to take a short power nap in the relative safety of the car. This *small* detail concerning my journey toward Åndalsnes will remain concealed until my return to the United States, as I'll purposely neglect to report it to both my U.S. and Italian families, thus avoiding any unnecessary concern for their solo-driving relative sleeping inside a car, in a remote location surrounded by woods, in a foreign country.

"A che punto sei?[71]" asks my mother. My barely awake brain quickly switches into alert mode, sending a "careful what you say, and for the love of God, do NOT look or sound tired!" message to all available synapses. Bless her heart, any time my mom calls me she raises the volume of her voice as if by doing so, she could allow me to hear her directly from Sicily without the need for any technology. But isn't that human need for closeness what makes vocal and video chats so beautiful and heartwarming?

"Un punto e una figura.[72]" I answer. "I just stopped by a restroom for a bio break."

She frowns, worried. "You look tired."

I move my phone around trying to find a more favorably lit setting. "No way, I had plenty of sleep on the boat. It's just the lack of light, as my phone is almost out of charge," I say. Luckily, I don't have any genetic connection with Pinocchio[73] or my nose, already sizable, thanks to my Greek ancestors, would sprint out of my skull.

"Don't drive too much today, please. Find a nice hotel. You can drive tomorrow."

"That's a good idea, mum. I think I'll drive another couple of hours and then I'll stop for the day. Don't worry." And there you have it. My windshield would have gone to pieces, crushed by my furiously growing snout. "All right, mom, I need to go. I'll call you later."

"Be careful. Drive slowly! Love you."

"Ciao, Mamma."

Guilty of having just delivered a bunch of white lies, I resume my journey south, and around 11 a.m. I cross once again Nordlandsporten, the gate that marks the border between Nord-Norge and Trøndelag.

Glistening under the bright sun, the funky and creative arch shaped to resemble the northern lights marks my official exit from Norway's northern regions. Since my landing in Bodø, I have already driven for about 562 kilometers (349 miles), and although Trondheim is still about 4.5 hours away, I'm perfectly on schedule, the weather is terrific, and I feel like everything is under control. *This is going to be a great day. What could go wrong?*

Nordlandsporten is not just a brick-and-mortar and political mark between two regions, Nord-Norge and Trøndelag, but also a cultural boundary between two ways of living. Behind me, I leave Nord-Norge, a vast land[74] bathed by full days of light in summer and cloaked by day-long darkness in winter. It is a territory shared by Norwegians and Indigenous Sami, where, until modern times, life was harsh, job opportunities were limited, and communications and commerce were only possible thanks to a strong network of sea routes. In Nord-Norge, I felt Mother Nature's strength when I wrestled Senja island's fierce winds to take pictures and drove through arctic lands designed by millennia of glaciers, or when I crossed a bridge built over a maelstrom of currents and slept soothed by powerful sea waves—which, now that I think about it, was probably not a very smart thing to do. But in Nord-Norge, I also experienced the heart-warming openness and honesty of people who would take the time to share details about their preferred photo spots, walk with me to the best restaurant serving king crab[75](and then laugh at me, feeling "crabby" for a golden missed opportunity), take the risk of allowing me to board their ship with just the promise of a later payment, or give up their own pen to allow me to write something nice about their homeland.

South of Nordlandsporten is Trøndelag, the most fertile region of Norway, home to generations of Viking leaders, and Frostating[76], the oldest known collective institution in Europe (1000-1600 AD). Personally, Nordlandsporten marks also my transition from a section of Norway I had never been before to a place I'm more accustomed to, having traveled across the region many times in the past. This is the closest place in Norway I can link to the Sicilian way of life and perception of time. Trøndelag is rich in culture and history, and comprises a diverse topography that includes large islands, high mountain ranges, and green valleys crossed by some of the best salmon rivers in Europe.

Most of all, Trøndelag is a place where time slows down and people live a very laid-back lifestyle centered on culture, arts, and family. Norwegians call this "Kos," a state of mind that centers on valuing the simple joys of life as if they were luxuries. And it's this kind of lifestyle that I experience when I stop by the Namsskogan's Circle-K gas station that also carries products made by local artisans. Realizing that I have neglected to buy something to take home to my family, I purchase a unique troll made with pebbles and some spices I have never heard of but that Hannah, the store manager, finds delightful when serving fish. Outside, the river Namsen flows slowly with its blue waters reflecting the sunlight.

I am sipping my Circle-K freshly brewed coffee and enjoying the view of the valley when I hear her voice. "Sir?" asks Hannah, the manager of the gas station. "Is everything ok?"

"Your credit card." You forgot to take it with you." She hands over my card. "Is everything ok? You look a bit…lost," she says.

"Thank you," I reply. Surprised by her outright and genuine ask, I secure my card inside my wallet. "Probably I am lost." I point out the idyllic scenery in front of me. "I mean, how could I not be?"

Hannah smiles and looks out to the valley. "Yes, it's beautiful." Then, with the serious tone I would have when reprimanding my kids, "Don't lose your credit card again!"

"Promise!" Obediently, I nod and walk back to my car.

That sense of belonging to a warm and welcoming community continues to surround me when I walk into a co-op facility to buy some food. The store is not just a trade center where local farmers can sell their produce, but it also functions like an indoor Italian *Piazza*: a place where people can sell their crafts, friends can get a cup of coffee and sit by a fireplace to catch up on the latest events, and newcomers like me can talk to locals and learn about the region. Eager to snack of some healthy food that does not taste like my usual chocolate and caffeine, I stock up on delicious strawberries I'll later immortalize in my portfolio of pictures, and on carrots so sweet they won't make it to the photo shoot at all.

A few miles south, I realize that the communal bond people share goes beyond the mundane timeline of the living ones. Harran Kirke is a simple white church built in the late 1800s that is not as famous as other religious structures like the Viking Stavkirke of Urnes or Heddal. Inside, its white and austere walls are not decorated with complex carvings of animals or sacred symbols, and its interior space has no trace of wooden artifacts intertwining the teachings and the blessings of old and new gods. But for the people of Harran, this sacred place, and the church that stood on the same grounds before being replaced by a larger, efficient building, represent a living cornerstone of the overall community. Testimony to that, is the perfectly manicured grounds and the caring reverence of a man tending to the tombstones of townsfolk who walked on the same land at a time when life was harder, some children would not live long enough to say their first word, and life expectancy was much shorter than mine.

I walk through the grounds for a few minutes, until a call from my family wakes me from my state of bliss.

"How is it going?" my husband asks, yawning.

"I feel like I'm standing in a place lost in time," I reply.

"Are you in Trondheim?" He's scrambling eggs, the sound of which triggers the smell of sizzling bacon in my brain

"Not yet; I am taking pictures of a beautiful valley."

"Nice. Are you at a panoramic rest stop?"

"Kind of. I'm technically walking in a graveyard." A sudden curse word coming from the other side of the Atlantic Ocean signals to me that my *chef* may have burned his fingers. "Are you ok? Why are you walking in a graveyard?" he asks. In the background, the sound of running water confirms my theory: he burned his fingers.

"Can you imagine their lives?" I reply. "They died so young. They had so many stories to tell. So many ideas for unwritten memoirs…"

"If you say so." Another curse word and the sound of something breaking into pieces on the floor. "I better wake up the kids. I'll call you later."

I look around once more. It's so quiet. "Sounds good," I reply. "Give them a hug." And I know that at some point I'll have to face once again the daily chaotic, early-morning kids' school routine. But I stand still for a few more minutes listening to the occasional sounds of the nearby river or the breeze brushing the leaves' edges… or just nothing.

- Namsskogan -

8

Just a Mess

AT SAUR (the farm located on lake Snåsavatnet, not the magical Viking dog[77]) everything goes sour. Clouds rejoin my journey, rain pours heavily, and construction work and large trucks slow me down. Any buffer time I had planned to invest in a formal meal in Trondheim is gone. By the time I reach the old capital of Norway[78], not only has my previous state of bliss dissipated, but I am tired, hungry, and quite stressed out.

The road infrastructure around Trondheim is impressive. After having driven on mostly one-way lanes for four days, Trondheim's three-lanes highway each way gives me the feeling of driving on an standard U.S. interstate. The only difference is that in Norway, here and there, large roundabouts facilitate the crossing of interconnecting roads. In the United States the same flow would be managed through a convoluted system of bridges or underpasses which would inevitably require more land appropriation and maintenance.

Returning to Trondheim[79] after three decades, is like stepping into a world that is familiar, yet transformed. As a student with plenty of time and limited financial resources, I stayed with friends for a couple of days near the Norwegian University of Science and Technology. It was cold, then, at least for Italian standards. Yet, students were rowing in the Nidelva river, regardless of the water's freezing temperature. Today, my scarce resource is time. Trondheim, the third largest city in Norway, is as charming, lively, and as colorful as I remembered it—and definitely larger than it used to be. Even on this gray, rainy and soggy afternoon, I can feel the vibes of a city that is cheerful and energetic; its streets and squares crowded with people strolling or walking in and out of restaurants, coffee shops and pubs. Fortunately, I'm able to secure a parking spot in close proximity to Torvet. Trondheim's main square and heart of the city, Torvet was completely refurbished between 2017 and 2020 to be more usable by its citizens[80]. The square is also the central crossing of wide streets specifically designed, after the Horneman Fire[81], to prevent flames from spreading from one part of the city to another.

Before leaving the car, I check once again my wallet, passport, phone, camera, and car keys. Everything seems perfectly in place.

Camera around my neck, backpack on my shoulders, and wallet in my right hand, I rush toward Torvet square while searching for a parking meter to pay for my parking space.

"Unnskyld meg. Excuse me," somebody behind me shouts.

I'm in the center of the square, taking pictures from a strategic location under Olav Tryggvason's monument. Had the weather been nicer, the shadow of Trondheim founder would have marked my lateness on a sundial laid out on the ground. I turn to find a tall man holding one of my camera widgets in his hand.

"It fell from your bag," he says pointing to one of the zips in my backpack. Apparently as I was rushing to get to the square the pocket had opened, and my camera device had fallen to the ground. "Be careful," he adds. "You don't want to lose anything valuable."

I thank him and promise to be more cautious. I check my backpack and then sprint to my next target, Munkegata, in several places capturing a few shots with both my camera and phone. Munkegata, named after the monks living by the cathedral, is Trondheim's main street and one of Norway's few avenues[82]. The road cuts the city in two, drawing an imaginary straight line leading from

Nidaros cathedral to the city's harbor, and to the island of Munkholmen lapped by the waters of Trondheimsfjord.

I sprint by the courthouse, Vigeland's "Red Deer Stag on Stone Ground" sculpture, the National Museum of Decorative Arts, and the City Hall. When I reach the gates of the Nidaros Cathedral's I stop, speechless. Either in awe, or simply out of breath, I stare.

Nidaros Cathedral[83] is not only the city's heart, but also Norway's national shrine and Northern Europe's main pilgrimage site—the northernmost Gothic cathedral. Built over the tomb of St. Olav Tryggvason, damaged by several fires, and subsequently rebuilt and restored through several projects concluding in 2024, the cathedral has been a permanent fixture of Norway's history for more than a thousand years. Every year, pilgrims from all over the world hike one of the nine trails crossing Norway, Sweden or Denmark to reach Trondheim, walk around the cathedral three times, and visit St. Olav's burial place set inside the cathedral. Thought St. Olav's Ways[84] or commonly Old King's Road, is less glamorous than El Camino de Santiago,[85] as just about a few hundred wayfarers travel through some of the most authentic and poignant historic and religious sites in Scandinavia, compared to the 200,000 people tracing the Spanish El Camino annually.

Walking the 640 kilometers (400 miles) path that begins in Oslo is in my bucket list, but it would require long planning and training for a person lacking the basic knowledge of some of the core skills required to hike for such a long distance. For now, my short run from the parking lot will have to suffice.

I drop my backpack on the ground, and I set my wallet, which I have been holding in my right hand since leaving the car, on top of a stone pedestal. I take a few moments to admire the craftsmanship of stone masons and glass makers, and I try to imagine how the church must have looked like at its peak of influence: a time when pilgrims from all over Scandinavia walked for hundreds of miles to reach this sacred place. With my camera and phone, I take a few shots; then, quickly, gather my belongings and run back to the car.

According to Google Maps, I could be in Åndalsnes in just a bit more than four hours. *The longest leg of my trip is almost over*, I think as I drive out of Trondheim. *As long as the weather holds for the next few hours, I'll soon have a nice dinner and a comfortable hotel room to sleep in.*

Little did I know I had just made a terrible mistake that would significantly affect the rest of my trip. Had I stopped for just one minute to check if everything was in order, I would have realized earlier the mess I had just created for me and the many people who would soon pitch in to help me.

As I drive south, rain intensifies, fog rises and roads narrow. I'm close to Innlandet, the only landlocked region of Norway—a region I visited at a time when Oppland and Hedland had not yet been merged[86]. I pause by a rest stop for a quick bio break, and once again I must face the reality that, in Norway, the astronomical start of fall is not just a season or a state of mind. In Norway, the September equinox, that special moment when the sun crosses the celestial equator, marks the time when many touristic attractions close, mountain passes are "Open depending on weather conditions" and rest stop bathrooms are "Closed for the Season," as specifically stated by visually appealing signs.

Drenched to my bones, I look up at the vertical walls of the surrounding mountains, whose tops are hidden by fog and torrential rain. "Darn, I forgot!" I loudly curse.

I'm not sure if I am more upset because the restrooms are closed and I need them urgently as the wetness of the clothes I am wearing, the drenching rain, and the overflowing river running nearby are not really helping, or because I realize that mountain foggy roads are going to require more time to reach Åndalsnes than what Google Maps idyllic journey had promised me. In the absence of indoor structurally robust facilities, and with the uncertainty of opportunities to stop anywhere up on the mountains, I quickly scan for possible alternatives. Under soaking rain, I pick the option that mostly applies under similar circumstances.

Back in the car, I quickly change into dry clothes, crank up the heater and distribute my wet apparel between my front and back passengers' seats. For some reason, I find the dismal condition of my car is humorous, and I make the mistake of sending a picture to my family in the United States—an action I immediately regret, as the replies are quick to arrive.

"Papa, are you ok?" asks my daughter. "Are you getting sick?"

"What?" is the only thing I can get from my teenage son.

"Did you lose your mind?" my gracious and supportive husband wonders.

I stoically move on. The road climbs uphill and the rain thickens. At an altitude of about 1,500 meters (4,900 feet), the woods disappear and leave the space to lichens, shrubs... and snow. The temperature lowers to below freezing and as if the visibility was not already inadequate enough, fog joins and the road becomes slippery. I can see only a few feet in front of me, and I have just a few hours of light left. *This is definitely not a place I want to drive through at nighttime*, I grumble. My car's stereo system sings "Hvorfor, Hvorfor." Although Emma Steinbakken's song has a quite different flair and meaning, the words "Why, Why," seem perfectly appropriate for the occasion.

Dombås is a key Norwegian crossroad. This small village set 610 meters (2,000 feet) above the sea, surrounded by natural parks and historical sites, is the point where the E6, on its journey north from Oslo to Trondheim, meets with Highway E136, a main artery leading to the west side of the country. This is also the place where the north/south Dovrebanen train line and its westward sibling Raumabanen meet. To me, Dombås appears through the fog as a long-awaited refuge and I ponder if I should just stop in one of the many charming hotels with panoramic views around the nearby mountains.

Perhaps because I want to get as close as possible to Trollstingen[87], a striking mountain pass I would like to visit tomorrow, or maybe just because my phone app lures me with the promise of reaching a nice hotel in Åndalsnes in about 90 minutes, I follow the E136 westward and enter the northern part of Gudbrandsdalen valley. Contrary to my app's estimate, it will take hours of rain and slow traffic before I arrive at my destination late in the evening. With no reservations made, I park my car outside Grand Hotel Bellevue and I check for room availability. Good news: a room is available and just waiting for me! I quickly put on my jacket and search for my wallet inside my pockets.

The wallet is not there.

It has always been inside my jacket!

Since I left the airport in Minneapolis, I have never been separated from it, and I've always kept it in my jacket. *Maybe it's lying on one of the floor mats?* I look for it everywhere multiple times. Nothing. I have lost it. Either it's somewhere in Trondheim, or I lost it when I stopped at the rest stop near the mountains, and it now lies on the ground in the middle of the woods. I imagine police officers leading people and rescue dogs on a search for some crazy Italian fallen (maybe it was suicide?) in the freezing waters of the nearby river; waters swollen by torrential rain. I sit silently inside my car. I've run out of cash, I have no credit cards, medical insurance cards—even my little dog's pet insurance card is gone. And so is my Lifetime gym membership card. (For some reason, the loss of my gym membership really bothers me—a membership I have not used since before COVID closings! But some way, I feel the immediate need of a hot yoga session followed by healthy, dairy-free smoothies.)

I need help.

"William." My call to my husband in Minnesota goes to voicemail. "Please call me. I need help. I lost my wallet, and I have no money to check in at the hotel."

I purposely avoid calling my Italian family. To inform Italians that I've lost all sources of financial security while driving on a solo trip in a foreign country, would be a call for disaster and a family tragedy the extension of which would reach all corners of the peninsula (and all national islands) in a matter of hours with an unsustainable load on telecom infrastructures.

I walk to the front desk.

"Are you ok?" asks Kari, the Hotel manager on duty. The reflection in the mirror behind Kari presents an image of myself that I hardly recognize: disheveled hair, puffy red eyes, and a pale skin tone. I look horrendous.

I'm in the process of explaining my situation to Kari, when William calls back. "Put me through to the front desk," he assertively asks. I avoid any talk and hand her the phone.

Kari listens to William and nods. "I'll make an exception," she tells me. "But I need you to understand. We don't usually take credit card payments made by guests who are not checking in with us." Then she gives me back the phone.

"Park the car, get your luggage in the room, and get something to eat," William says. His tone is firm and direct. "Call me after dinner."

I follow the instructions and stop by the dining room just in time to order something before closing time. Eating is therapeutic; it helps me think rationally about what needs to be done. First, I need to accept that the wallet is lost. It's either seven hours north, somewhere in Trondheim, or it's buried under thick foliage in the middle of the woods.

Next, I need to figure out a way to make it to the end of the trip—or at least reach Oslo, where I have friends who can help me. When it's time for the check, Ingrid, the server, asks if I want to charge my dinner to the room or if I want to use a cardless payment.

The boat from Moskenes to Bodø! My brain cells finally activate. I could have (and I should have) paid for the ferry with a mobile payment app.

"How would that work?" I ask Ingrid.

"Some companies allow you to move your card to the wallet from the app. For other ones, like AMEX, you would need the real card."

I follow the steps required to add my credit cards to my Google wallet. Two of my credit cards require a physical card, which of course I don't have anymore. I have one last chance: my US Bank card. I look at Ingrid: "Do you mind if I take a few minutes to try?"

"Of course, take your time," she says.

I hope she really means it. It's almost midnight and I'm quite sure she would prefer to be home, instead of having to deal with an Italian who carelessly lost his wallet.

I open the app of my last credit card, and there it is—a link to add the card to my Google Wallet. *Eureka!* I rush to Ingrid to test my first mobile payment. The first couple of attempts fail miserably. *Maybe if I remove the phone cover... Bingo!* Transaction accepted.

Excited, I hurry to my room. "I have access to money!" I tell William. Of course, my extremely rational partner of 20+ years, instead of celebrating my relief with me, goes on detailing a long list of "what if" scenarios should I neglect to cancel my credit cards as soon as possible. And just to add interest to my already messed-up situation, he adds: "Are you sure you can always use your phone to pay for your purchases?"

I freeze. I have less than half a tank of gas left. *What if I can't find a gas station that allows mobile payments?*

"You there?" I hear.

"Yes, I'm here. Let me cancel my cards," I reply. "I'll call you back."

It's past midnight. All the gas stations around the hotel are probably closed but, just in case, I leave the hotel looking for a gas station that accepts mobile payments. First, I try all the large brand gas stations like Total and Chevron. Nothing. I need a physical credit card.

I stop by the last remaining gas station: a Circle K. The very same family of gas stations that employed the Finnsnes' gas station manager who gave me his own pen and the Namsskogan's service station manager who come out of the station to return the credit card I had left at the cash register. I cross my fingers and position my phone by the self-service machine. Transaction accepted! I load the car with gas.

I try my luck once again and I stop by a few banks hoping to withdraw some cash. But I've asked for too much. Cash Withdrawals are not allowed.

Back in my room, with just a few hours left before sunrise, I evaluate my options. I could wake up at 4 a.m., drive to Trollstingen and Geiranger, cross some of the most panoramic mountains in Norway, and risk running out of gas before getting to Flåm, my next destination. Or I could drive back north to Trondheim to find my wallet. At some point in my thought process, I transition to deep sleep, R.E.M. mode. I guess I'll figure it out tomorrow.

- Driving South -

DAY 6

Galdhøppingen

9

High on Hope

I'M DRIVING A CONVERTIBLE through Namsskogan. It's warm and sunny and the back of my car is loaded with fresh strawberries and carrots. The air smells of French lavender and seagulls fly over the car. Their chirp is pleasant, at first, but gets louder and louder until I wake up at the thought of Hitchcock-style birds in attack mode.

But it's just my phone. "Did you lose your wallet?" screams my Italian sister. I wish I were still driving through Namsskogan, but reality hits. "Why didn't you call us?"

"How do you know?" I ask. I'm puzzled. Maybe my husband called my Sicilian family and shared the news?

"Facebook."

"Facebook? Ma che dici, what are you taking about?" I try to change the topic.

"I received a Facebook message from a lady in Norway. She found your wallet."

"What? Where?"

"Cretino! Idiot! It was somewhere in Trondheim. Your ID was inside the wallet. She searched for you on Facebook, figured out I am your sister, and sent me a note on Messenger. You are lucky. She is a nice person."

"This is incredible." With new hope, I start packing.

"I sent you her contact information. Make sure you call her SUBITO—RIGHT NOW!"

"Thank you."

"You bet. Now I'll put you through to mum."

"No, please!" I beg. The image of a Greek/Roman Fury pops up in front of me.

"You deserve it. For not calling us earlier!"

Still only half awake, I explain to my mother how I may have lost my wallet in Trondheim, maybe while I was rushing from one place to the other.

"Call me on your way to Trondheim." Her voice is sharp and direct. "Please be careful."

And as abruptly as the conversation had started with my sister, it ended with my mother. After a quick breakfast and a few exchanges with Marit, the guardian angel who found my wallet in Trondheim, I am on my way back north. It would take me about six hours to get to Trondheim, with no time to drive back to Trollstingen, Geiranger, and finally Flåm in time for the last train. My two-day stop in Myrdal will have to wait until my next opportunity for a trip to Norway.

I leave Åndalsnes and drive through the luscious, green Romsdalen, one of the most beautiful valleys in Norway. To my right, is the winding Rauma River and Trollveggen, the *Troll Wall*, the tallest vertical rock face in Europe with its 1,100 meters (3,600 ft) of gneiss rock. When I pass the old Marstein train station, I look up to Mannen, *The Man*, mountain, and think about the valley residents, who live under the constant danger of rockslides.

Every now and then I stop by a few curbside parking spots to exchange messages with Marit, trying to agree on a time and place to meet. The short breaks also allow me to take pictures of the valley. And even though I am anxious to reconnect with my wallet and recapture the sense of security I have lost, the peaceful sight of the green valley, the clear waters of the Rauma River, the flocks of sheep grazing in the fields set me back to a sense of rational calm.

A few miles south of Dombås, William calls. "Why don't you call your friends in Oslo? Maybe they can help you."

"How?" I ask. "They will probably wonder how stupid I was."

"Well, of course they will."

"Thank you. Now I feel better."

"Listen to me," he persists. "They are still your friends, and they love you. Maybe you could ask Marit to arrange for the wallet to be sent to Oslo. You could just pick it up on your way back home to the United States on Friday."

I must give him credit; William can always come up with simple but smart ideas. "You know what?" I reply. "That is why I love you."

"What?" he replies, followed by a giggle.

"You can be rational in the most irrational situations."

"Glad I am useful for something, I guess."

"It's actually a great idea. Let me call them."

"Bye, crazy."

"Ciao. I'll keep you posted."

I stop by a cliff and text my friend Turil in Oslo. When I explain my situation, Turil offers an even better solution. Her daughter Liv lives in Trondheim. I just need to send her Marit's information in Trondheim. Liv will meet with Marit to pick up the wallet and will overnight it to Oslo where I'll be able to pick it up on my way to the airport.

"Thank you!" I exclaim, relieved that I don't have to drive up north and cross the mountains once again. (How naïve of me. I didn't have a clue what was ahead!) "Don't worry," Turil replies. "Just enjoy your trip. I'll see you in Oslo in a few days."

I evaluate two options. I could drive back to Åndalsnes and follow my planned path via Trollstingen and Geiranger. But once in Kaupanger, I would have to cross Sognefjord by boat, and I still have no credit cards or cash. I was able to board without a credit card in Moskenes, but it's better not to risk getting just a few miles from my next destination only to be forced to drive around the fjord to reach it.

***

"DRIVE TO DOMBÅS," suggests Øyvind, owner of the B&B in Myrdal, a place where I am longing to rest for a couple of days. "If you drive through the southern side of the fjord, you'll find Tindevegen[88]. It's a mountain road, a bit rough, but if you follow it all the way downhill, you'll avoid crossing the fjord."

"That sounds like a great idea, I say." I quickly scan my paper-based map, trying to find any indication of a road called Tindevegen. When I finally identify a small path through the Jotunheimen mountain range, I nod. *How bad could it be?*

"All right," I tell Øyvind. "We have a plan. See you for dinner."

"Don't forget to stop by the grocery store."

"Not a problem. Tindevegen looks like a nice shortcut. I'll have plenty of time. Ha det!"

"Ha det bra. See you later, Daniele."

I hop in the car, and at Dombås I turn south to follow the Gudbrandsdalslågen river, a path that has been the main route to Nidaros (today, Trondheim) since Medieval times, and the most popular of the nine St. Olav Ways pilgrim paths[89]. Taking such a journey on foot would be a once-in-a-lifetime experience. But hiking from Oslo to Trondheim would take about a month, and at this moment I am not able to entertain such an idea. There are a few things that I can do, however, to have a taste of that emotional journey, like stopping by a couple of quaint villages and symbolic landmarks along the pilgrims' path.

Nord-Sel is the settlement that impresses me the most. Its Viking style, dark brown wooden church is stunning in its simple and timeless beauty. Every year, set near the front gate of the church, a statue of Kristin Lavransdatter[90], a fictitious 14th-century hero of a Norwegian literary trilogy by Nobel Prize winner Sigrid Undset, welcomes thousands of pilgrims looking for shelter, food, and some rest on their way to Trondheim.

Before leaving the Nord-Sel Kirkje, I say a prayer for the people buried in the cemetery and under the WWII memorial that protects the bodies of 31 soldiers (one of them unidentified).

I resume my journey. "Here Comes the Rain Again," Annie Lennox sings. And yes, the rain is falling as I drive on Fylkesvei 438, cruising through small farms, thick woods, and flocks of sheep filling the land between Sel and Vågåmo. It's damp, wet, and foggy when the turquoise water of Lake Vågåvatnet strikes me with its unbelievable hue. This is one of the entry points to the Jotunheimen, *Home of the Giants*, mountain range. I can easily imagine giant creatures visiting the enchanted Lake Vågåvatnet to freshen up and restore after having fought a bloody war against other gods. Jotunheimen is an area of about 3,500 sq kilometers (1400 sq miles) encompassing most of the tallest and sharpest mountains in Norway and a multitude of glaciers that have been grinding rocks for thousand years into a fine glacier flour. In spring, summer and early fall, as the glaciers melt, the waters carry the fine silt downstream to lakes like Vågåvatnet. The silt remains suspended in the waters and absorbs part of the light's spectrum of colors, reflecting only the blue tones.

In a sense, I must be thankful for the rain, as it has allowed more silt to flow into the lake. The more the silt, the more intense the color. (There you have it: a glass half full!) But for some reason, I can't drink this glass of Kool-Aid because I still feel wet and damp as I take pictures and short videos. And when I get back to the car, I sneeze.

Darn! I don't have any prescriptions with me. I change into dry clothes as I beg all gods, mine, and the Valhalla ones, to keep me healthy at least until I get to my destination in Myrdal. Hoping to not get a cold and for better weather, I set the wet clothes to dry in the backseat and I resolve to be more careful when taking pictures out in the rain as I have only one clean change of clothes left.

Rain continues to pour and mindful of my time constraints and worried about my sneezing, when I reach Fossbergom, at the conjunction of the rivers Otta and Bøvra, I skip a stop by the Lom Stave Church, one of the largest stave churches remaining in Norway. Instead, I continue my journey turning on Sognefjell National Route[91], one of Norway's most fascinating scenic routes.

Even under a steady rain, Sognefjell Roads's sinuous and slow climb uphill through green meadows and lush farms lining up through the Bøverdalen Valley is captivating.

"How is it going?" asks my worried husband on his "just-to-check-on-me" call.

"Pretty good," I lie. I'm quite nervous at the idea of traveling without any significant source of funding. "The drive is easy."

"Good. Try not to drive too much today.

"Isn't it a bit early in U.S.?"

"Yeah," he says, yawning". I couldn't sleep."

"Go back to bed. I promise I'll be at the B&B in a few hours."

"Ok. Drive safe."

"I will. Good night!"

In the far distance, thunder rumbles. Or maybe it's just the gods laughing at me from their colossal palaces up on the towering Breheimen mountains on my right and the Jotunheimen peaks at my left. Meanwhile, totally oblivious to me, the Bovra River, with its powerful rushing waters, carries more silt from Bøverbrean glacier down to Lake Vågåvatnet. In a few days, the sun will finally glisten on the lake, the turquoise hue will be spectacular—although I won't be there to enjoy it. If shades of blue are not in my immediate future, at least I can immerse myself in a sea of green tones. From the dark green of the pine trees, and the bold jade of the thick grass covering the pastures, to the gray-green tones of lichens attached to the rock formations.

Driving through Bøverdalen is like journeying through a land of Tolkien's elves living in beautiful castles hidden in the woods. And so, it does not surprise me to find small, charming hotels along the way built around structures hundreds of years old and recognized by generations of Norwegians. They are the Røisheim Hotel, previously a post station since 1858, with structures dating back to 1700s, or the 1800s family estate Hotel Elveseter with its Sagasoylen, a 34-meter tall (105 feet) stone column designed in the early 1920s to become the new national monument of Norway and later set aside after its sculptor supported the German invasion during WWII.

A part of me begs to stop at one of the hotels to have a scrumptious meal, but the rational part of my brain pushes me to follow Sognefjellroad, every left turn gifting me with a glimpse of Galdhøppiggen, the highest mountain in Norway. The road narrows and the vegetation decrease at every mile uphill. It gets colder and colder until it's just snow and ice all around me. I've reached 1,428 meters (4,600 feet) above sea level, and connectivity is scarce. I constantly lose satellite radio and my navigation system freezes here and there. When the road ends at a closed gate leading to a narrow, metal bridge, I wonder if my paper-based map would be sufficient to guide me through the mountains should I completely lose satellite coverage.

* * *

I LEAVE THE CAR TO SURVEY THE GATE. Luckily, it's not yet closed for the season. I open it, cross the bridge and stop. I may not be on top of the world, but I've reached the top of Europe's highest mountain pass. And it's beautiful! Deserted, quiet, icy, bare, and disconnected from the rest of the world, this place is indescribably stunning.

- Sognefjellet -

10

Uphill, Downhill, and Up Again

"ATTENTION, SEASONALLY RESTRICTED ROAD AHEAD," announces my navigation system.

The Styggedalsbreen glacier is behind me and connectivity is still spotty, although getting better by the minute. A red light guards another narrow bridge. And I wait. Even though I can clearly see that there are no oncoming vehicles, I wait. Even though there is nobody around to maintain the light and it has probably been red for the past few hours, and there is no certainty that it will ever become green again, I wait. According to my navigation system, I'll arrive at the train station in Flåm with plenty of time to take the last train to Myrdal, so I have time. Time to stop and smell the roses. Or, in my case, smell frozen, cold moss. If that's even a thing.

The light finally turns green, and I'm allowed to enter a new section of Sognefjellsvegen, still barren and desolated but spellbinding at each turn. *Had I not lost my wallet, I would never have driven along such a scenic path.* Laughable thought: should anything happen to the car, this would probably be the worst place to be. I'm rarely passing any vehicle at all—a sign that probably I should not be driving on this road this late in the season— and connectivity is almost nonexistent. Even if I still had my wallet with me, what good would that do to me on such a lunar-type, isolated landscape?

Similar thoughts and other random considerations help me keep moving on. With no satellite coverage, thus no soundtrack to keep me company, and a breezy cold wind *inspiring* me to stay inside the car instead of taking pictures in the wilderness, I've plenty of time to connect with my *inner self*. And my *inner self* and I agree: we are a mess. If acknowledgment is the first step to redemption, we (me, myself and I) are on a good path.

By the time I arrive at Hotel Turtagrø, it's lunchtime. Whatever coffee I have left from my gas station shopping spree in Dombås is ice cold and I've half of a rosin ball and few chips of chocolate left on the passenger seat. *Maybe I could have a quick meal at the hotel.*

Hotel Turtagrø, in some shape or form, has been welcoming travelers since the late 1800s, when farmer and reindeer hunter Ole Berg and his wife Anna settled in the area[92]. Of the two original structures that used to make up the hotel, only the Swiss Villa still exist today, rebuilt after a fire almost burned it to the ground in 2001. I stop by its restaurant to check the menu.

"Darn! The restaurant closed at the end of August. I guess lunch will have to be my half rosinboller bun."

At Turtagrø, Sognefjellsvegen crosses with Tindevegen, a dirt mountain road. If I drive straight, Sognefjellsvegen will take me to the northern shores of Lustrafjord, the innermost branch of Sognefjord. To cross the fjord and reach Flåm, I'd have to take a ferry. Without a credit card, I risk getting stuck at the crossing point, just a few miles from my final destination. If I turn left on Tindevegen, the "shortcut", as my B&B host Øyvind called it, will take me to the southern branch of the fjord, thus avoiding the need for a boat crossing. *I'd be able to reach Flåm with enough time to buy groceries for my two-day stop in Myrdal.*

With no cars behind, I'm not in a rush to make a choice—a choice that seems easy, as long as I don't mind the quality of the roads standing in front of me.

The narrow Sognefjellsvegen, with all its limitations, looks like a large interstate compared to the one lane gravel path that marks Tindevegen. All of a sudden, my navigation system comes back to life to show me how close I am to the fjord. The rough mountain dirt road, Tindevegen, seems like a bumpy but short nuisance between me and the valley lying down below by the fjord. With complete disregard for the road sign posted at the entrance of the path, I turn left on Tindevegen, a man-made blend of tight hairpin bends, steep climbs, treacherous 90-degree turns with no visibility whatsoever of what is coming from the opposite direction, and some of the most incredible views I have ever seen in my life.

At one very memorable point, I find myself almost at a dead stop as the road sharply turns to the left and narrows to its extreme leaving just a small gap between a large rock protruding from the mountain and a cliff leading to Valhalla.

Seriously? I shout to the giant gods of Jotunheimen, and once again I regret driving a long station wagon. I take a big breath, blast my car's horn, and follow the road. A few drops of cold sweat cross my face when I reach the other side of the curve. I'm still alone, rocks lined up to my left and feet of ... nothing to my right.

It takes me a long time to drive the 15 kilometers (approximately 9.5 miles) between Turtagrø and a toll station—an actual, physical toll station with solid bars stopping the traffic ahead. Because naturally, after driving for days around Norway without encountering any physical barrier at all, it makes perfect sense to find a toll station on top of one of the highest mountain ridges in Europe, with nobody in sight to help. And one thing Øyvind, the navigation system, and Google Maps did not mention is that I need to insert a physical credit card to get through the gate!

Still hopeful, I walk to the guard post and knock at the door, but nobody answers. It's the end of the tourist season. What are the chances that a wandering tourist with no credit cards would show up at one of the few remaining toll gates left in Norway looking for help? Even I, myself, would rate that possibility as insignificantly low and not worth assigning on-site personnel. My only option is to drive back to Turtagrø, follow Sognefjellsvegen to the ferry dock, and hope for some good Samaritan to pay for my crossing.

Somehow, I make it back to Turtagrø. A few meters before the crossing between Sognefjellsvegen and Tindevegen, a sign covered by dust and mud (the one I did not bother to read earlier on) captures my attention.

"Kun Kredittkort."

Credit cards only? You must be kidding!

Any memory of my treacherous return journey on Tindevegen has been thoroughly erased from my hippocampus. The weather finally clears up when I turn onto Sognefjellsvegen. The road is narrow, but its paved surface is a welcoming upgrade compared to Tindevegen. Soon the appearance of green vegetation and trees signals that I'm slowly weaving downhill. At Fortun, I stop by a small, white church to take a short walk. If I had phone signal, it would be a good time to *call a friend* and wait for my blood pressure levels to get back to normal. Instead, I hop in the car and move on to my next priority.

I am almost out of gas.

* * *

THE SKY TURNS TO THE MOST REMARKABLE SHADE OF BLUE. Maybe Fortun will bring me luck[93].

The road to Kaupanger is very relaxing and pretty much empty of drivers, except for a few residents. This section of Sognefjellsvegen meanders through green pastures and small villages. Here and there, waterfalls drop down to the valley feeding a web of streams that flow into Sognefjord.

I finally reach Kaupanger and its docks. Ironically, I could have just as well kept to my original travel plan and driven through Trollstingen and Geiranger. The only reason I drove through the mountains was to avoid the crossing of Sognefjord. Well, here I am, tired and hungry, in the same spot I've tried to avoid all day. As I wait for the ferry to arrive, I process a few scenarios: I could beg for money, ask the boat's crew for a later payment, or sing a song and collect donations.

The ferry arrives and drivers gradually board. I get in line, hoping to find an understanding agent who is also open to listen to a distracted and naive Italian tourist with no wallet.

Arne welcomes me onboard and guides me to my assigned spot. "Enjoy the ride," he says. Then he moves to the next traveler.

I'm an idiot! The airport rental car agents had explained it to me very clearly. But at that time, I was too wired up and ready to go on with my adventure, to carefully listen to their words. In Norway, transits via ferry are like entering road crossings (except for the toll gate on Tindevegen, of course). A picture is taken at the time of boarding, and a bill is sent to the owner of the car. My original plan of driving through Trollveggen and Geiranger would have worked perfectly.

But what about the beautiful mountains, the views, and the thrill of the unknown? asks my inner self. The glass is always half full!

Evidently, my inner self and my rational being see the *glass* in different ways right now. And specifically, the rational self would rather have a glass of red wine.

While the ferry crosses Sognefjord, I call Øyvind to let him know I'm on my way.

"I'll just stop by the grocery store," I tell him.

"Too late," he replies. "If you don't get to the train station soon, you'll miss the last train."

"But I'm crossing the fjord, and I have almost two hours left."

"You are on the boat, and you still have to land," says Øyvind, with his precisely descriptive and technically correct way of talking that should have given me an idea of his personality. "Once you land, you still have to drive through Lærdalstunnelen, the longest road tunnel."

"The longest road tunnel in Norway, or in Europe?" I reply, not really grasping the dimension of what I am about to drive through.

"In the world. It's 24.5 kilometers (15.2 miles) long. Don't fall asleep while you drive, and make sure you don't speed, either. There are plenty of speeding machines inside the tunnel."

"All right." It's the only thing I manage to reply. "I'll call you from the train station."

Following Øyvind's advice, I skip any possible distraction, and I try to stay alert for the entire drive through the tunnel. Opened in late 2000, Lærdalstunnelen is the longest tunnel in the world. The last time I visited the region, the tunnel was still under construction and there was no ferry-free connection or dangerous mountain crossing during winter season between Oslo and Bergen. Today, hundreds of vehicles take advantage of this completely tool free, stunning marvel of civil engineering set between Aurland and Lærdal. Once inside, it feels like being in a space designed to endure an apocalyptic catastrophe. Occasionally, the monotony of the tunnel is broken by enormous round spaces that resemble the square of a large city illuminated by intense purple neon lights. As I would learn later on, it's a strategy to keep the driver alert.

I reach the Flåm's station just 10 minutes before the departure of the last train to Myrdal. No time for grocery shopping or the purchasing of a few alcoholic beverages. After all I have been through, a nice glass of Kentucky Bourbon (or a shot of Aquavit) would be really welcome.

Boarding has already begun when I get to the ticket office. In front of me, a couple of tourists are evaluating with Ida, the only customer service member on duty, all possible opportunities for entertainment.

"This is too long of a trip," assertively states the husband to his wife. He points to a different option and shows it to her. "What about this one?"

"Too expensive," She replies and turns to the train station's concierge. "What would you do if you were us?"

Ida is evidently tired of having to deal with demanding tourists and is probably looking forward to ending her work shift, but with a very *Minnesota nice* attitude, she says:

"Both options are good. Perhaps, I would choose this other tour, though. It's not too long and it's nicely priced."

"I don't know..." answers the wife.

"Excuse me madam," I say, taking advantage of that short break in the conversation and I channel a mix of polite Norwegian and frustrated/tired Italian temper. "Would there be another person I could work with to buy a ticket to Myrdal? The train will leave soon."

"Of course." Ida calls a colleague who quickly helps me with my ticket.

I rush to the platform, just in time to hop on the train before its departure. Once on board, I set my backpack and hand luggage on the floor, and I sink into the plush seat of the Flåmsbana[94]. The cushioned embrace feels like a long-awaited relief. As I settle in, eyes closing briefly to savor the moment, a strange but profound sensation begins to unfold. It's a feeling of shared exhaustion and solace, an invisible thread that connects me to countless others who have sought refuge in this very seat; a collective, silent camaraderie with fellow passengers who, like me, have been seeking a moment of peace midst the bustle of their lives.

The Flåmsbana is one of the steepest (5.5% gradient for most of the trip) standard-gauge railway lines in the world. During its 20 kilometers (12.4 miles) journey, the train passes through a series of hand-drilled tunnels, snow roofs and breathtaking views of dream landscapes, lost-in-time villages, and spectacular waterfalls. The realization of the steepest railway line in Norway in a terrain that presented many engineering challenges, required the sweat and hard work of hundreds of workers who spent about 6.1 million man-hours to complete the track. The construction works also ignited economic development in Flåm, Myrdal, and the surrounding region; places that would have been otherwise scarcely populated. The Flåmsbana attracted construction workers, cooks, blacksmiths, engineers, horse owners, horse police[95], and doctors. People built lives and got married, built homes, post offices, a school with a swimming pool, long distance telephone exchanges and general stores.

This train car is more than just a vehicle where my bum sits on a surface that has welcomed many other derrieres; it's a sanctuary built in recognition of the immense human effort behind this simple act of sitting down and resting. It's a place where fellow travelers can join in the collective weariness of countless laborers who laid the tracks, engineers who led the construction work and designed the train, maintenance crews who kept everything running smoothly, and workers' family members who, since 1924, joined in the dream of realizing the Flåmsbana. I am finally relaxing.

I've got nowhere to drive to, no turns to take and no decisions to make. I just must get off the train at Myrdal. *How challenging can that be?*

* * *

I'M ENJOYING THE VIEW OF THE MOUNTAINS when the train stops, and my phone vibrates.

"Where are you?" Øyvind asks in a dry, serious and inquisitive voice.

"On the train, enjoying the view. I almost dozed off," I say.

"Get off the train."

"Now? But I am not in Myrdal yet. The train just stopped in the middle of nowhere."

"Of course the train stopped," Øyvind answers with a Norwegian-kind, severe but still ironic tone of voice that I can't really figure out.

"We are all waiting for you to get off the train!"

I look outside, and there he is. Øyvind is waving at me. The train manager, standing nearby, is tensely checking his clock. I gather all my belongings and apologize to the other guests traveling on my same car. Some of them, laughing, wave. Others nod, annoyed.

I get off the train and thank the train manager. He assesses me head to toe. I'm wearing Italian dress pants, a white shirt, trainer shoes, and a light jacket. In my hands a small trolley and a map of Norway. He snorts lightly. I feel his disapproval. I am one of those naïve tourists who have no business in being here.

"Hi Øyvind, great meeting you in person!" I say, trying to break the silence that hovered over the station's platform.

"You were supposed to stop at Reinunga."

"I'm so sorry. I thought I was going to stop at Myrdal." I apologize, feeling like a high school student who failed his test.

"No, I told you to get off at Reinunga. You are lucky the train engineer knows me. That's the reason why he stopped the train."

"Oh. Well, I'm ready for the adventure. Let's go."

"No."

"Why?" Now I'm lost. I don't know what to do.

Øyvind looks at me, all dressed up as if I'm ready for a walk in the middle of Florence, Italy. He looks me in the eye and states once again, "No."

"Excuse me?"

"You need better shoes. These won't work."

Øyvind is wearing hiking clothes and boots, and I suddenly remember that per his specific request, I had to leave most of my clothes at home to dedicate half of my hand luggage's limited space to a pair of bulky hiking boots. "Ah! My boots. They are inside my luggage."

"You need to wear them from now on."

Øyvind shows me the way to the small storage room that also serves as waiting room for the train station. I quietly change inside the warehouse and follow my guide into the unknown.

Once we leave the Reinunga train station, I find myself entering a magic place. We follow a path of wooden planks, natural rocks and colorful moss and lichens. (And as a reminder to myself, never bring a trolley in the woods! Woods are no place for items with wheels. Unless they are carriages, of course.) We walk across the dam that holds the waters of Kjosfossen, the waterfall I had taken pictures of just a few minutes earlier, and finally we reach Øyvind's delightful property.

The original construction dates back to the time when Øyvind's grandfather supervised the construction of the Flåmsbana and, as the leader of his community, took care of his team of workers helping with the construction of barracks (and paths leading from one edifice to the other), settling disputes, and even lending money when needed.

Øyvind stops by the porch of his hytta. I gaze out at the breathtaking valley spread before me. The serene lake Reinungavatnet shimmers under the late September golden afternoon sun, its surface reflecting an azure sky dotted by small, cotton candy clouds. Beyond the lake, dense woods stretch out, their summer green covers already changing into shades of brown and red tones.

"Can you see those cabins downhill?" Asks Øyvind, pointing to a few structures nestled among the trees.

I nod in silence.

"They belonged to the workers who helped build the Flåmsbana. My grandfather was the leader of this small community and lived in this hytta most of his life with my grandmother and their children."

"Are the original owners of the cabins still living here?" I ask.

"Not really, they are mostly all rented."

Øyvind welcomes me to his cabin. Once he inherited it, he expanded the original building and added modern amenities, some of which, like chairs, tables, and wall accents, he personally crafted or designed.

"How did you bring the fridge and the dishwasher up here?" I ask. "There are no roads."

"Easy," Øyvind answers. "I waited for winter when the lake freezes. As all appliances come in pieces, I put the parts on the train from Oslo. Once in Reinunga, I loaded them on a sledge which I simply pushed through snow and ice."

I wait for a moment before replying, just to make sure he is not making fun of me.

"The heavier elements of the house, however, like the water tank, or the lumber I used to build the expansion of the hytta, needed some additional help," continues Øyvind.

"I can imagine." Is the only thing I came up with as a reply. "So, what did you do?"

"Ingen problem, a piece of cake. I rented a helicopter."

"Of course," I mumble. "That sounds just like the right thing to do." I reply, as I try to imagine me and my husband pulling a sledge full of parts across a frozen lake or directing a helicopter. *Why not?*

Øyvind shows me his workshop and the tools he used to craft many features of his hytta, including his cedar wood-fire hot tub overlooking Lake Reinunga. Then he opens the door to what will be my room for the next two nights.

"What do you think?" He asks.

The large windows on two of the room's walls open directly to the lake. The sun is setting, and all around the valley, everything is covered with a golden hue. "Stunning," I reply.

I just have time for a quick change of clothes when Øyvind calls me for dinner. It turns out he is also a great chef, and his deer soup is superb. One of the great things about spending time with somebody who lives in the places you are visiting is that you can learn things you'll never learn anywhere else. Øyvind is an engineer, a craftsman, and a bee farmer. *I can't wait to try some homemade honey tomorrow morning for breakfast.* During dinner, while a try to limit my consumption of freshly baked bread, we talk about social and political developments in Norway, Italy and the United States, innovative approaches to address global challenges (e.g. energy, immigration, responsible fishing...) and his view, which I also share, that regardless our own personal political views, we still need to reach a compromise.

"At the end of the day, we need to solve the most compelling issue we are facing at that specific moment and move on to the next challenge."

After a refreshing and energizing rinse in the outdoor shower attached to the outhouse—the water comes directly from a nearby waterfall—it's hot tub time. Øyvind has built by himself a round, cauldron-shaped hot tub heated by a wood-burning furnace set on an elevated panoramic platform overlooking Lake Reinungavatnet. The evening air is cool and crisp and the scent of burning wood is soothing.

"My grandfather hired most of the workers who built the Flåmsbana," says Øyvind as he adds more wood to the furnace. "When I was a child, I used to spend all Summer with my grandparents here in Reinunga. We would spend the days exploring the woods, picking berries, preparing food and meeting people. But the time I cherished the most was when we would gather to listen to the stories of what used to be a very vibrant and close community."

The sky is clear, for once, and the starry night would be an ideal backdrop for witnessing the northern lights. Careful not to spill water on the furnace, Øyvind gets into the tub. We float lazily on the surface of the hot tub seeking the warmest pockets of intensely hot water.

"I heard stories of workers digging tunnels in the mountains almost by hand," says Øyvind, suddenly breaking the silence. "I could tell you who was born in which cabin, who got married where, who was the best chef and to whom my grandfather loaned money."

"I can understand why you are so attached to this hytta and Reinunga," I say. "It's part of who you are."

The heat is relaxing. The hot water wraps around me like a soft blanket, melting away today's tension. Silence and the starry night sky envelop the valley.

Life is good.

- Road to Flåm -

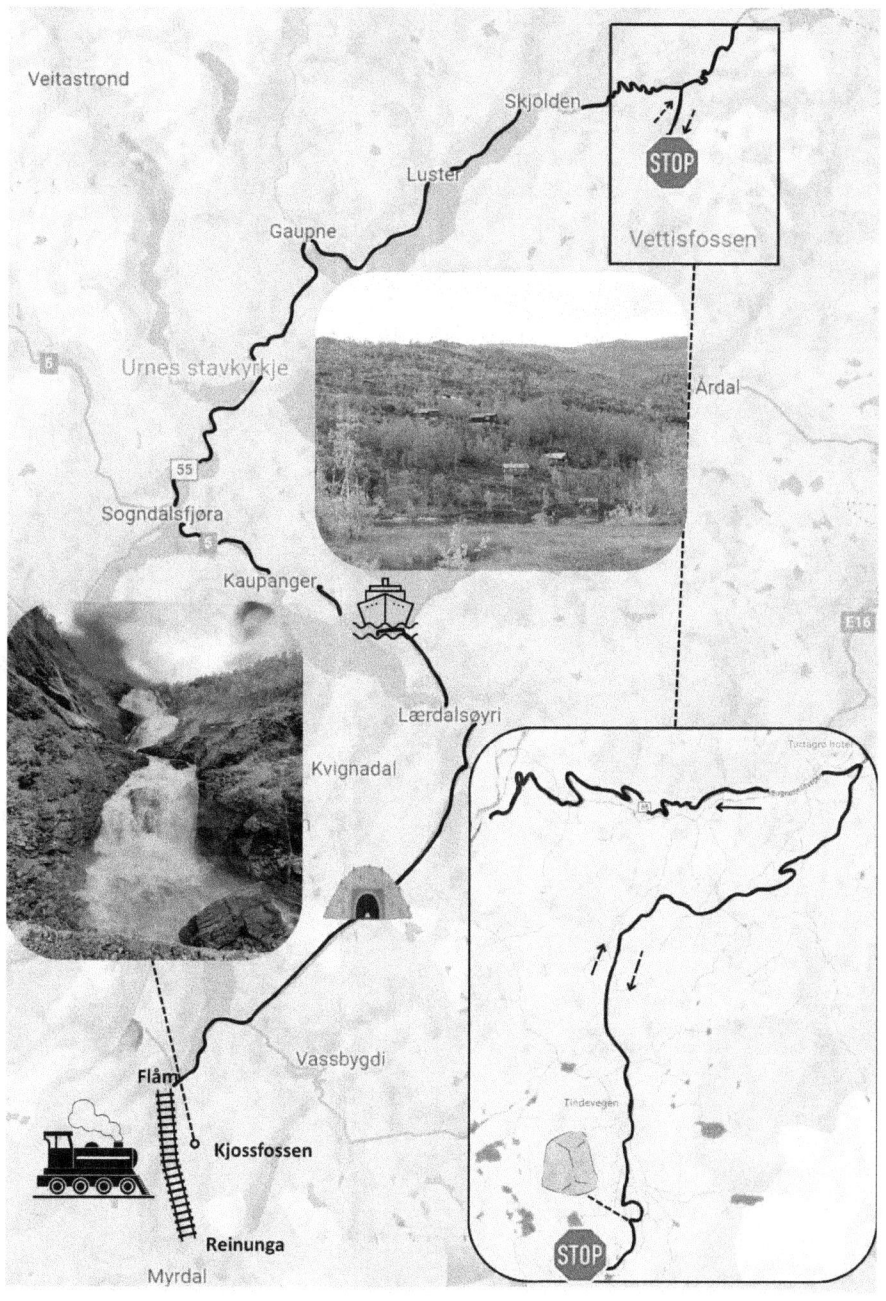

DAY 7

Reinunga

11

Reinunga

I KNEW FROM THE BEGINNING that my journey would be a whirlwind of excitement, but also a frantic and tiring endeavor. Anticipating the need for a respite, I had planned a one-day break to breathe, relax, and reflect on everything I had experienced so far. Dawn breaks gently over Lake Reinungavatnet. From my bedroom's floor-to-ceiling windows, I gaze out at a spectacular sunrise. The sun casts a golden glow on the serene waters of a lake that transforms into a mirror reflecting the emerging colors of the sky and the Fall tones of the surrounding woods. In the background, the first light of the day brushes with a warm, rosy hue the tall, ageless mountains.

A mountain hike sounds like the perfect thing to do today.

"Time for breakfast!" calls Øyvind.

I enter the dining room to find a table that is a delightful feast for the senses. At the center, a large platter holds a variety of deer and elk meats. To one side, a basket with homemade warm bread, a jar with honey, and a bowl with fresh handmade berry jam[96]. Boiled eggs rest in a warming dish just next to something I had longed to taste again for a long time, gjetost!

Gjetost, which can be translated with "goat cheese," is not really cheese. When making cheese, milk is broken into curds and whey. While cheese derives from the curds (fat and proteins), gjetost originates from the whey component, and it tastes like sweet and salty caramel. Some people may not like it but I'm quite addicted to it.

Especially if I can spread it on top of fresh, homemade bread and top it with berry jam.

"Looks like you like it," exclaims Øyvind, pointing to the big chunk of gjetost I'm eating.

"What gave it away?" I respond with a laugh.

"What are you planning to do today?" Asks Øyvind.

"I have been sitting inside a car for days," I answer. "I'm thinking about a hike."

Øyvind nods. "Good idea."

The kitchen is filled with the comforting aroma of fresh bread. I'm thoroughly enjoying slice after slice of honey-soaked bread and gjetost topped with berry jam while Øyvind shows me on Google maps a path leading up a few mountains and three different lakes.

"Are you listening?" Asks Øyvind, noticing that I'm more focused on licking my honey-drenched fingers than on looking at the Google map he has set on my phone.

"Of course, of course." I reply as I clean up honey that has found its way on my shirt and pants. *How difficult can it be? I just need to follow the path as indicated on my phone.*

I mentally split the journey into four different stages: a way for me to set both achievable and stretch goals. I know, the purpose of this trip is to not have goals or schedules or plans, but my project manager/engineering brain is constantly on alert mode, I guess.

Before I leave, Øyvind gives me a bag with sandwiches, Lunsj chocolate, some gjetost, and a thermos full of hot tea. "You'll need this for your hike," he says.

"It looks like the survival kit for somebody going away for days," I chuckle as I accept the bag.

"Something like that. Maybe just enough to get you going, considering your appetite at breakfast time."

"Point taken," I reply. "But in my defense, I've not had gjetost in decades!"

"The wind will pick up as you climb uphill." Øyvind nodded toward the mountains in the background. "The thermos is well insulated. Hold it with your hands when you get cold. It will keep you warm for hours, I promise."

"Thank you, Øyvind," I set the thermos inside my backpack. "And thank you for helping map my itinerary."

"Well, about that." Øyvind slowly shakes his head from side to side. "You must take a picture of it before you leave."

"Why? I have it on Google Maps."

"You can open Google Maps because I have set up a hotspot in the hytta. Walk a few yards out and you'll be cut off."

I pause for a moment, weighing the implications of his statement. I immediately regret having given more attention to my honey-soaked sandwich of gjetost and berries than to Øyvind's detailed directions on how to get from one point to the other.

"What if I get lost," I ask. "Will I be able to call or text?"

"You may or you may not. I guess you better don't," Øyvind giggles. And considering that this is the first time I see him laughing, I suppose he is having a heck of a time thinking of a inexperienced Italian hiker lost in the woods.

"Fine." I take pictures of the itinerary with my phone and show them to him. "Am I good to go, now?"

Øyvind gives me a thumb's up "Text me when you are on your way back. Oh! I forgot. You won't be able to." He laughs again. "See you later!"

"Whatever," I mumble.

* * *

I LEAVE THE HYTTA AROUND 11:30 A.M. *It's a late start for a long hike but I have no other choice.* The weather does not look promising. It's cloudy, cold, and really damp, but I don't mind. I hold the warm thermos in my hands and move on. This is my time off from everything and everyone.

According to Øyvind's instructions, the hiking path begins at the Reinunga train station, just a few yards away. Interestingly enough, the toughest part of the journey is actually finding my way back to the train station itself. The path between Øyvind's cabin and the station is really just a collection of wooden planks, moss trails and rock paths through which I must figure out my way by following an imaginary *southern* direction. This nature-made maze is puzzling but full of fantastic photo opportunities, reflection moments, and "what the heck" exclamations in all the five languages I know.

It *only* takes me about 45 minutes to find a gravel path leading to the hiking trail. A day earlier, guided by Øyvind, it had taken less than 15 minutes to trace the exact same itinerary. I can finally stop worrying about where I'm going. I just need to follow the trail and enjoy the beauty that surrounds me: the waterfalls, the bogs, the vegetation of giant ferns and colorful moss and lichens, the rock formations, the boat stored under a rock, the bike laid on a deserted field of ferns, and the empty buildings. I could write dozens of stories just taking inspiration from what I am looking at or the few hikers I pass: the French biker looking for a good spot for his tent, the maintenance workers driving up and down the path, and the divers looking for fish.

Many years ago, while I was living in Kentucky, any time I drove the children to daycare I noticed a man walking on Dixie Highway: his head bent down on a small book. I don't know if that was a Bible, a notepad, or some other manuscript or sacred text, it doesn't matter.

The point is that I always wondered why he did it. Why did he need to walk and carry something to meditate or write on? And now I get it: while walking, you get many creative ideas and thoughts. Your mind just goes free, and you know that unless you capture those moments as they happen, you will lose them forever.

The notepad I've been carrying all week is halfway full of notes, mostly related to the first part of my journey. It also includes feelings and thoughts of what I can achieve in the next few years, both personally and professionally. I stop to write by the Styvedalsgrovi and the Setregrovi Rivers, their waters rushing from small waterfalls on the sides of the Geitanosi mountain. I sit on a rock in the middle of the woods, with thick moss, purple lichens, and giant ferns all around. Service is extremely scarce and sporadic but, lucky me, as I listen to the sounds of streaming rivers and birds, I get enough service for T-mobile to successfully send me a note to remind me how much I have spent on international roaming call charges. It's not much, but did I really need that message right now? I set the phone on mute and take a step forward on the rocky gravel path, cherishing the memories of the past few decades.

The more I walk uphill, the more beautiful the views. At about 2:30 in the afternoon, I find the perfect place for lunch: a terrific rock formation overlooking Lake Reinunga with an open viewpoint that allows me to see as far as the snowy caps of the Tarve and Geitanosi mountains. My home-made honey sandwich and my pickles, deer meat and cheese panino just feel delicious in my mouth. When the sun finally finds its way out of the clouds, a Lunsj chocolate melting in my mouth, I feel like I'm on top of the world.

The weather is unpredictable and a fresh drizzle reminds me that I need to get moving forward and uphill to reach beyond Kaldaklovfossen and Lake Seltuftvatnet. The woods offer some cover for a while, but once I reach the Moldåni gorges, I'm too high up on the mountains for any tree to grow. Random bushes and lichens cover the rocky slopes. To add to the fun, a cold wind starts blowing and a thick layer of clouds cover the sky. I wish I had brought gloves and a warm hat with me. Luckily, my thermos is still warm and the hot tea has never felt warmer and more soothing.

"Is this the way to Myrdal?" asks Pierre, a French biker. Pierre has been biking on mountain trails since early in the morning.

"Yes, you are on the right path. You'll ride downhill, first. But for the final stretch you'll have to climb a bit," I tell him.

"That won't be a problem. I've biked through harder paths since I started in Haugastøl, 80 kilometers south." Pierre takes a sip from his water bottle. "Where are you heading?"

"Back to Reinunga. I had a nice hike." I answer. "But I'm thinking about turning back to have some dinner."

"Keep on going. Trust me, the next lake, Klevavatn, is something you don't want to miss. Once you get to the railroad, walk through the gallery and you'll reach Klevavatn."

"Well, thank you for the tip. I guess dinner will have to wait, then."

I follow Pierre's suggestion, and I move on until I reach the railroad, and the hiking path suddenly stops. The railroad leads to a cluster of buildings on the right and a tunnel on the left. Before me lies the expansive Lake Klevavatn. *Did Pierre bike through the tunnel? That would be madness. There must be another way.* I walk back downhill, and to my left I notice a small gallery that looks more like an unlit, upgraded bat cave than a real trail. I take a deep breath and enter the grotto, hoping for the best.

It's wet, dark, and slippery. Droplets of water fall from the jagged ceiling splashing into shallow puddles on the ground. With mixed feelings of anxiety and curiosity, and anticipation, I accelerate my pace. The cave soon turns right toward a dim light, and as the exit approaches, the darkness slowly reveals a stunning view.

Lake Klevavatn is spectacular, even on a cold, gray and rainy day. I take in the serene and majestic scene, and I realize that for the first time in years, I feel at peace. After all the driving to get to my target destination, the rushing to find the perfect picture opportunity at the right time of the day, the sleepless nights spent cruising to stretch destinations, and the stress and anxiety of having to drive and live with limited access to money, I've finally found a place where I can be absolutely at peace with myself.

What's next? asks my inner self.

For now, nothing, I smile.

* * *

THE WATER IS CALM AND CRYSTAL-CLEAR. The air is fresh and filled with earthy scents of wood and moss. I sit down by the water's edge; eyes fixed on the peaceful scene surrounding me. After a few moments, I pick a smooth, flat pebble from the shore and I toss it across the surface of the lake. The rock skips once, twice, then disappears into the blue watery depths leaving nothing behind but fading ripples that quickly smooth out like they never existed. I throw another pebble. And then another one.

When I was younger and I still lived in Sicily, I met a psychic and palm reader. I was very skeptical, as I have always been pretty much a rational, "everything-is-based-on-science" person. But still, I went through the process. The palm reader told me many simple things that later became reality. Or as I always say, I associated them with something that happened in my life, and I perceived them as a true prediction. One thing she told me, though, was so odd and so unachievable for the person I was at that time, that it caught me off guard. The palm reader looked straight into my eyes, and with a surprised and questioning look, told me that I would have a long life but that my heart would be split in three pieces, each one living in a different place. At that time, as a high school student, I had never left the island of Sicily except for our summer family trips to neighboring regions of Southern Italy or, occasionally, to visit our relatives in Torino, near the French border in the north of the country. I never thought I would ever leave the island.

But life took me on unexpected journeys, and as my birth family stayed on the island, I traveled, lived and worked in different places, including Norway, before finally landing in the United States to build a family of my own. Maybe the palm reader was right. Or maybe, once again, my brain is trying to find an association with what she told me. Italy, and Sicily in particular, is the place where I was born, raised, and taught how to behave, love and tend to people. It's the land that gave me the foundations of who I am today. It's also the place where my large and loving birth family and my childhood friends live. The United States is the land that taught me how to live and build an independent, financially solid, and socially constructive life. It's also the place where I've realized a family of my own and new friendships. But in this dichotomy between my old life and the new, between the responsibilities linked to handling the needs and expectations of two families on two separate continents, one thing has slowly dwindled: my own self.

What the palm reader told me, is not something that is specific just to me. We are all trying to do our best to answer everybody's needs and give parts of ourselves here and there to make sure that our loved ones, our friends, and our co-workers are happy. In the end, little or nothing is left of ourselves. Maybe Norway is my third place. A spot just for me. A land I can come to for a few days each year to explore places I have not yet experienced, to share a meal with friends and talk about history and traditions, or just to learn how to deal with my own quirky, naïve, and at the same time rational and somewhat unpredictable self. A small boat approaches from a distance. The lake is now silver-gray, and clouds returns to shield the sunlight. For me, it's cold and windy once again. But for the two men laughing on the boat, this must be just an opportunity to have a great time together, regardless the meteorological conditions.

I've spent enough time journaling and meditating. I must get back to Øyvind's cabin if I want to make it by sunset. With no signal, I better avoid getting lost in these woods and bogs in the dark. Luckily, most of the hike back home is downhill. My legs hurt badly. I'm out of shape and spending four days sitting in a car did not help. Once again, I get lost between the Reinunga train station and Øyvind's hytta. I barely make it to the front door before dark. Waiting for me, a great display of food featuring Indian curry rice with homemade bread and berry jam. An after-dinner dip in the hot tub is the perfect closing for a day to remember. I check my pedometer: 25,273 steps.

- From Reinungavatnet to Klevavatn -

DAY 8

Seltuftvatnet

12

På Gjensin Eden

MY OFF-THE-GRID TIME IN REINUNGA IS ALMOST OVER. Before leaving, I take a short hike to climb the rocks onto which some of the beams of the B&B are drilled. Just a few feet above me is the waterfall that feeds the outdoor shower. The view is terrific. I take a moment to enjoy the surrounding nature and beauty, and to listen to the sounds of waterfalls, birds, and the wind weaving through bushes and trees. I feel the warmth of the sun on my skin. I smell the wet moss, the rotting birchwood, and the purple wildflowers blooming on the ground. I taste the droplets of water free falling from the waterfall nearby (and hope I won't get sick). I inhale the air deep in my lungs as if I could take that feeling with me forever.

"Daniele, time to go!" My rational, straight-to-the-point Øyvind reminds me.

After taking some more pictures of Lake Reinunga, I get back to the hytta to find a new display of homemade bread and honey, wild berries jam, cuts of wild game and, of course, gjetost. I thank Øyvind for the great experience, for sharing his views of the world, and most of all, for paying for my return ticket to Flåm.

Leaving Reinunga is tough. I've spent less than 48 hours in this sheltered scenery, but I feel changed, even though I can't pinpoint exactly how. My hand luggage feels some kind of change as well. As I pack, the back of the suitcase gives away and I'm left with two separate shells, like the two pieces of an open European hard-shell kinder egg[97]. (Unfortunately, no chocolate was identified after the accident.)

Boots, jacket, and backpack on, I walk back to the train station precariously holding in my hands the hand luggage as I make my way through wooden planks, bogs, and large boulders.

As expected, I get lost once again. After *visiting* a few other cabins, luckily empty, and finding myself at the end of paths leading straight into Lake Reinunga, I finally make it to the train station in time to remove my hiking boots and put on my sneakers. And in a transformation that takes only a few minutes, I mutate from a vision of "wild-and-free-breaker-of-rules Daniele" to my usual, ordinary-lifestyle self. But inside, I'm still changed.

I'll find a way to keep this feeling alive, I think, as the Flåmbana takes me back to Flåm. I look around and it's quiet. In the almost surreal silence, I realize that most of the passengers share the same lost kind of look. Gone is the excitement experienced on the way uphill, when looking forward to reach our own destinations up in the mountains, we all looked like little children laughing at each other and exchanging seats from one side of the train to the other on our own quests of taking as many videos and pictures as possible. Lunden, Håreina, Berekvam, Blomheller, Reinunga, Vatnahalsen, Myrdal, to us travelers, they were just different names for the same utopian location: Heaven.

As we descend back to Flåm, instead, we are all silent: a stillness occasionally broken by the rhythmic clattering of the wheels as the train slowly moves along the tracks. We are all lost in our thoughts gazing out of the windows in an attempt to freeze in our memory places and adventures that will soon be behind us. På Gjensin[98] Eden.

It takes only a few minutes to reach Flåm. My car, waiting in an empty parking lot, has a full tank of gas. I could easily venture east to Stegastein viewpoint[99] or Lærdal and its Borgund stave church.

"Why don't you drive directly to Bergen?" my husband texts me. He's up early again to get the kids ready for school. "If the banks are still open, you may be able to talk to a teller and get some cash. Or maybe one of the cash machines will allow you to make a withdrawal with your phone app."

Once again, he is right; I should stay focused. I pick up my itinerary binder and scratch out Stegastein, Lærdal, and Borgund. But at the same time, I highlight a few great stops along the way to Bergen. "Good idea," I text back.

I press the ignition button and turn west toward Bergen. And just because I spent two days surrounded by natural beauty, it seems fair that the first part of my journey to the west coast of Norway should begin with an underground drive through the Gudvanga and the Flenja tunnels. I had passed through the Lærdal tunnel, the longest tunnel in the world, a couple of days earlier to reach Flåm, and now I drive through the Gudvanga tunnel, the third longest in the world. The three tunnels together cover 43 kilometers (about 27 miles) of the 51 kilometers (32 miles) between Gudvangen and Lærdal. This system of three tunnels drilled through some of the most magnificent mountains in the world is the only winter-safe road between Bergen and Oslo. A couple of decades ago, when I last visited Norway, it would have taken me about seven hours and two ferry connections to reach Bergen. Thanks to the new system of tunnels, I'll be able to be downtown in about three hours. I just need to be careful driving for a long time in a confined (very confined) space that feels as if it's taking you down to the core of the planet.

The good news is that the tunnel's designers have planned a few nuggets of entertainment (and safety) here and there to keep the drivers alert. Inside Lærdalstunnelen, for instance, three large roundabouts are lit by large blue light chandeliers hanging from the top of the cave, while yellow lights set at the bottom give a sunrise feeling. And if you like numbers, you can track your progress by checking the markers posted at each kilometer, stating how long you have driven and the distance remaining to the end of the tunnel. The Gudvanga tunnel, instead, is more austere and a bit older (and slightly more dangerous). It doesn't have the fancy blue light fixtures of Lærdalstunnelen, but you can still find a few sections lit with purple lights.

Driving underground may be gloomy and stressful, but once I cross the tunnels and I arrive in Gudvangen, I am rewarded with the superb view of Nærøyfjord. The threads of waterfalls dropping from the surrounding peaks are a welcoming sight in an elven-like land that echoes with water-made spilling sounds. This dreamlike branch of Sognefjord, Norway's longest fjord, has been listed as UNESCO World Heritage Site for its natural beauty. Its steep mountains, dotted by small farms clinging to the edges of the ocean, provided the inspiration for the creation of the town of Arendelle as featured in Disney's movie production of *Frozen*[100]. I make a note in my binder to return with my family and spend time here to rent kayaks, visit the Viking village and stop by Gudvangen's fish restaurant.

After spending two days in an idyllic place, I don't feel stressed anymore. I'm like a log carried to my destination by a slow and steady current. I follow upstream the Nærøydalselvi river. Steep mountains tower over the valley and cast shadows on farmlands and villages whose names date to the earliest ages of Norwegian history.

The E16 gently climbs uphill until I reach the border with Voss County, the "Adrenaline Capital" of Norway[101]. Voss, home of imposing mountains, breathtaking waterfalls, rushing rivers and miles of stunning biking and hiking trails, has been a hotspot destination for thrill-seeker enthusiasts of extreme sports such as water rafting, bike racing on the mountains or ski diving. Decades ago, to the risk averse, analytic, and in somewhat boring twenty-something version of me, Voss was the place where I discovered less hazardous, but more comforting culinary discoveries of rømmegrøt[102] and pinnekjøtt[103].

The E6 now runs through a plateau high enough to let me enjoy the glorious sun, previously hidden by the crests that sheltered the narrow Nærøydalselvi Valley. I am not the only one bathing in sunlight. Joining me is a sea of cows, goats, and other farm animals lounging leisurely on thick green pastures that seem to extend forever. Unexpectedly the emerald grounds end in the soothing blue waters of Lake Oppheimsvatnet where an old, white church watches over the village of Oppheim and its souls resting in the nearby cemetery.

Lake Oppheimsvatnet ends (or begins) at the mouth of the Strandaelvi River, and as soon as I turn right on a section of the European Highway 16 that cuts through the mountains, I get stuck behind a farm truck for a kilometers. The experience makes me laugh, as it reminds me of the many times I've had to drive at 30 or 20 miles per hour behind a *Lapa*[104] in Sicily, my homeland.

The truck driver finally allows me to pass him, and for a few miles I can drive at a decent speed until after the village of Vinje, the road narrows again to less than two lanes and, with no median line anymore, I slow down to safely give way to the fast-driving trucks coming from the opposite direction

During one of my evening hot tub conversations with Øyvind in Reinunga, we ended up talking about driving habits of Italians and Norwegians.

"We do NOT speed in Norway," the rules-driven, rational Øyvind stated decisively. "The speed limit marked on our signage is not a *suggestion*. It's the law."

"Sure," I say nodding. "But have you tried to tell the truck drivers?"

He looked at me puzzled for a moment, then giggled. "You are right."

"And I can tell you," I went on, "if the road is too narrow for me to give way to a gigantic, fast driving, horn-beeping truck, I'd rather get a fine than be hit!"

We both chuckled.

Once I reach lake Lønavatnet, the road widens again, allowing for a nice and relaxing drive through Voss, the large Vangsvatnet Lake and the more peaceful Seimsvatnet Lake, and the peaceful village of Evanger. I'm in a good, optimistic mood, so even though I still have only my phone app to access money, I still stop by the Dale of Norway outlet store at Dale.

I bought my first Dale of Norway sweater almost three decades ago on my first visit to Norway. Many years later, that Telemark region-inspired clothing item is still beautiful and perfectly functional. Following my first purchase, for the next five years, any time I went to Norway, I bought more items for my parents and my sister. Now that I am back in Norway, it's time for me to share my love for this brand with my family in the United States.

I enter the store and stop by the front desk. "Do you accept mobile payments?" I ask.

"Of course," the store manager answers. "Have you purchased any of our products before?"

"Yes. I bought my first Dale sweater almost 30 years ago."

"You mean thirteen?" she asks, puzzled.

"No, no. Tretti," I reply in Norwegian.

"What does it look like?" Helga asks.

"Well… it's a bit hard to describe," I say, looking around for items that may slightly resemble the one I own. I finally point toward the wall opposite us. "Actually, it looks like the one in that old picture over there. See? That sweater."

Helga startles. "That is quite an old picture. We don't make them anymore."

"Well, I guess I'll have to find something similar for my family at home."

"Take your time. Sounds like you know your way, around. Let me know how I can help."

Christmas presents for the family loaded in the car, I can now drive the last few miles to Bergen, the second largest city in Norway and rainiest city in Europe, with its 239 average rainy days per year[105]. For once, luck is on my side; the sun shines brilliantly in a clear, blue sky when I get to my hotel in Bryggen, Bergen's historic harbor district.

I enter the lobby, still with no physical form of payment.

It's not a problem, I think, as I've already paid for my reservation before leaving the United States. But when I stop by the front desk to check-in, it's clear that Sigrid, the hotel front-desk agent, does not share my point of view.

"I need a credit card to confirm your reservation," she says.

"But I've already paid for the room. Why do you need one?" I reply.

"I still need it. I'm sorry."

"Do you accept mobile pay?"

"I'm sorry. We do not," Sigrid grins with a Mona Lisa-like expression that is a combination of melancholy, contentment or like my kids described it, simply "I really don't care."

Without many options left, I call home. Maybe my husband can rescue me once again.

"Everything ok?" he asks.

"Not really. Even though I already paid for the room a couple of months ago, the hotel still needs a credit card."

"Can I pay with my credit card?"

"Excuse me, Sigrid, can my husband pay for me with his credit card?"

She looks at me, then checks around. "Is he with you?"

"Well, we are together of course. We are married," I joke showing her my ring. "But not TOGETHER, like in the same place right now."

Sigrid doesn't flinch. Either she doesn't care about my joke, or she doesn't like my answer. "No, he can't."

"What's happening?" yells my impatient other half.

"She is checking," I lie to him, trying to avoid having to entertain a phone conversation with a frustrated partner while at the same time keeping a nice and positive attitude with Sigrid.

"Sigrid, I lost my wallet in Trondheim and I don't have a physical credit card with me. Is there anything you can do? I've already paid for the room," I explain to her.

"Well, if you have a picture of the card, you could input the card numbers on the keypad."

Bingo, I think, then turn my attention back to my impatient other half. "Can you send me a picture of your credit card? I can input the digits in the machine."

"That doesn't make any sense. Isn't that the same as me giving her my credit card information?"

"I know. It doesn't make any sense, but we can argue about it later,"I say. "Can you please just send me the picture?"

"Fine. But I can do something even better. Your new AMEX just came in the mail. I'll send you pictures of your own card."

It only takes the time to input the information into the credit card machine to make Sigrid happy. The successful transaction magically lifts Sigrid's spirit. "Welcome to our hotel. Here is your room key."

I hold room card dearly as my most precious possession. And even though I am due for a really long, hot shower, something I've not had since my hotel stay in Åndalsnes, I quickly leave my belongings in the room and set course toward a group of banks where I hope to find someone who will help me getting cash with my phone app.

Bergen is a vibrant and colorful city especially when the sun shines. Restaurants, coffee shops and stores are filled with tourists and local citizens enjoying the afternoon. I walk through different neighborhoods and one by one, cross off my list the banks that are already closed. I'd arrived at the hotel by 4 p.m. but my interaction with Sigrid had shortened my window of opportunity. On the bright side, I have a room and I can charge a hotel dinner on my card. By tomorrow afternoon I'll be reunited with my wallet.

I've been to Bergen many times in the past. In many ways, the city is still the manicured, clean, and energetic one I remember, but a few things are different, as well. With the opening of the indoor fish Market, Mathallen, the merchants have a year-round indoor space to comfortably sell their products. Last time I was in Bergen, the vendors crowded the main pier with all the colors, sounds, shapes (and smells) that outdoor fish markets bring. Norwegian, family style restaurants were easier to find, and stores had more Scandinavian, non-touristy or mass-produced merchandise. But maybe it's just me and my nostalgic memories.

Before going back to the hotel, I stride through some of my preferred neighborhoods: the network of old narrow, charming streets leading to the Cathedral, the modern vibe of the shopping district and Torgallmenningen square[106], the massive St. John Catholic Church, and the octagonal Lille Lungegårdsvannet Lake surrounded by Bergen's colorful park.

Even getting lost in the maze of charming streets around the University is pleasant and fun, at least until hunger calls. Then it's time to get back to the hotel, put on some nice clothes (for the first time in a week) and get some delicious Norwegian cod and halibut at the hotel's restaurant.

Back in my bedroom, having completed a cycle of shower-enabled laundry washing, I discover the good and the bad of choosing a hotel located where the local action is.

If you want to socialize and network into the late hours, a hotel situated by the pier offers an ideal location in the heart of the city's popular hot spot. However, if your wake-up call is at 3 a.m., you need to go to bed early, and your bedroom is on the boardwalk... You are exactly in the heart of the city's hot spot!

Even the irresistible allure of my extremely comfortable bed and pillows can't make up for the loud squeals of inebriated younglings and a newly engaged couple's loudly proclaimed promises of never-ending love for each other. I manage to fall asleep to be awakened by even louder (and more inebriated) cries over a broken relationship. Apparently, during my short meeting with the goddess

Nótt[107], the loving couple must have had an irreconcilable (at least for the moment) argument which ended the engagement festivities with a break-up. For a while I try to re-engage my connection with the Viking goddess of the night, trying to ignore any cry of a broken heart. Eventually, I give up and get ready for a new day.

- From Reinunga to Bergen -

DAY 9

Hardangervidda

13

Road to Hell(e)

AT 2 A.M. I'M READY FOR THE LAST LEG OF MY TRIP —a journey that will take me through another stunning portion of Norwegian countryside all the way to Lillestrøm, where old friends, and my wallet, will meet me at lunchtime.

Needless to say, the clothes I had washed just a few hours earlier are still wet. The only thing I can do is to carry them to the car and set them to dry on the back passenger seats. Again, my car looks like the fancy residence of a digital nomad.

Circle K rescues me once more. Just outside Bergen I find a gas station that allows mobile payments. I load up with a full tank, just in case. And my judgment will be proven true: there will be no other opportunity to refuel the car until I reach the outskirts of Oslo, eight hours later.

There is always a strange feeling overcasting anything you do for the last time. Your last dinner in a special place; the last time you visit a city; the last chance to say goodbye. I've been running so much during the past few days that I didn't realize I've already had many firsts and lasts, every single day. I've stopped by dozens of cities, both large and small for the first and the last time. I've had meals at many gas stations (I know!) and a few restaurants for my first/last time. And now, for the last time, I'm driving my car to the next destination. I'm excited to see my friends in Oslo and to regain possession of my wallet, but at the same time I'm sad at the realization that my solo journey is coming to an end. And yes, after more than a week driving mostly at night, I've not been able to see the northern lights. Even tonight, although the sky is clear, there is no trace of one of the most spectacular natural events of the Northern Hemisphere.

I'm way ahead of schedule, the weather is supposed to be nice, and I have a full tank of gas. Nothing can go wrong, right?

Helle, Hordaland, which should not be confused with any of the other six cities called "Helle" in Norway, or the other 10 homonymous towns spread all over the world nor the Helle brand of Norwegian knives, is a cheerful village located at the mouth of Hellestraumen, a small branch of the fjord Veafjorden[108]. I would have probably never heard about Helle, Hordaland, or passed by its tourist facilities with picturesque names[109] like *Salmon Paradise, Fishing Paradise*, and *Secluded Fjord Harmony*, if it weren't for something that, after having driven across Norway for a week, I can call the "5 a.m. Rule": always assume that all road work will end at 5 a.m. sharp.

Usually, any nighttime roadwork ends up with traffic flow being regulated by a person or a light in a short section of the road. The effect would just be slower transits and reasonable delays, but nothing major. Sometimes, however, as I had experienced near Bodø, tunnels get completely shut down until, as the rule states, the magic hour of 5 a.m.

Just a few miles from Helle, a gigantic truck overtakes me, driving at a speed way faster than the speed limit. It's just the two of us on the road and there are no streetlights. For once, I actually welcome the additional set of headlights in front of me. It makes me feel less lonely and a bit safer. Although I doubt the truck driver would bother to turn around if anything happened to me.

The truck gradually gains terrain and for a while it seems that I'm soon going to lose sight of it.

I'll be driving alone once again, I think.

Suddenly, the truck slows down…and eventually stops. I do the same.

We may have to wait for upcoming vehicles to pass through. It won't take long. I try to reassure myself.

The *Jeopardy* jingle starts ringing in my brain and a few minutes later a small car with flashing light stops to my right. Olav, the driver, instructs me and the truck driver to follow him.

With the feeling of a 21st Century Alice in the Wonderland[110] threading on the heels of a white rabbit as it finds its way underground, the truck driver and I follow Olav and his service car through a couple of tunnels on a path that zigzags from one lane to the other as workers fix wire cables and other infrastructure on one side or the other of tunnels and roads. After a few minutes of twists and turns, Olav stops at the entrance of a tunnel, U-turns his vehicle and rests next to my car.

"Can we move forward?" I ask.

"No. The tunnel is closed until 5 a.m."

If I wait until 5 a.m., I'll never make it on time for lunch with my friends in Oslo. "Is there another way to get to Oslo?" I ask.

Olav pauses and looks at my car. Norwegians always have a direct answer, may that be a yes or a no, which is completely different from us Italians. We, Italians, try to make everybody happy and avoid confrontation, when possible. Mostly, we circle around the question thinking that a direct, negative answer would be too much of a burden for the listener to bear.

"You could drive back to the first exit and take the old road to Helle."

My tired brain does not translate Norwegian correctly and I reply in English. "You want me to go to Hell?"

Olav laughs loudly and I realize too late that he may have interpreted my question with the religious meaning of journeying to some underground place where souls are devoured by eternal flames. The truth is that I actually thought Olav wanted me to drive all the way to the town of Hell, Trøndelag; a village that I had passed a week earlier on my way to Trondheim. "No, not Hell." Olav manages to say this between one laugh and the next. (And by now I am laughing, as well). "Helle!"

I follow Olav to the exit and then turn right on Hellevegen for what will be one of the most electrifying segments of the entire trip.

* * *

I SHOULD HAVE KNOW FROM THE BEGINNING that Olav's pause wasn't because he was pondering different options. He knew exactly that the only way to avoid the tunnel was to drive through Helle. His hesitation stemmed from his mental assessment of the likelihood of an Italian tourist successfully navigating a long Volkswagen Passat through Hellevegen, suitably named "The road to Helle."

Hellevegen is a road so narrow that in many places my car barely fits. And just to ensure that vehicles stay within the concrete boundaries of the road, both sides are marked by big boulders, wooden fences, buildings, and safety barriers designed to reduce the chance of a possible fall downhill to an unfortunate encounter with a railway or the Dalevågen fjord. To make the journey more electrifying, in certain sections the road was literally carved into the mountain and massive, irregular walls of stone edge the passage giving the feeling of driving through an unfinished tunnel (or a partially collapsed one) whose roof dangerously flanks the rooftop of the car. When Hellevegen ends into a rock wall and turns sharp ninety degrees into a tight metal bridge over Hellestraumen, every sensor of my car yells. After some tricky maneuvering and a few expletive words in different languages, I manage to cross the Hellestraumen with no damage to the car.

But the fun is not over yet. My next challenge is to cross a railroad track. The warning lights are flashing, but the boom barrier is open. Unsure about the contradictory circumstances, I wait. Time passes by but no train approaches. Eventually, I see the lights of another car coming from the opposite direction.

Whatever they do, I'll follow, I think. The car slows down, stops, and then crosses the railroad. I make the sign of the cross, check to my left and right, yell up to my lungs, then put my foot on the accelerator and speed over the crossing. After a few more miles of narrow paths and menacing, irregular boulders threatening my car from both sides and above, I finally end up in a very large, industrial parking lot.

My relationship with the car's navigation system, which I named Sigrún[111] has been complicated since the very beginning. For the past eight days, we have been debating on which road would be in the best condition or which path would be faster. At some point, Sigrún directed me to cross a water mass to get from one side of a fjord to the other. Me, being a rational person and understanding that cars like mine are not amphibian and, as such, could not survive the drive through the ocean without the help of a boat, I declined Sigrún's suggestion—a decision that may have brought our relationship to a breaking point.

Regardless of what our bond had been before driving through Hellevegen, once I enter the parking lot, our relationship reaches the point of no return. Sigrún directs me through different trails leading to a railroad track, another parking area, and a warehouse. Tired of being manipulated by an AI device with whom I can't argue effectively, I decide to ignore Sigrún, and I turn toward the most lit-up area, which ends up being a gas station on the main road.

It would be a perfect time for a coffee and some food. But this is not a Circle K gas station and with no cash or credit cards, the only thing I can do is to stop by the restroom to refresh myself and reclaim some sort of mental balance.

I'm back on the European E16 and the sight of a median lane could not be more welcomed. A sense of calm envelops me inside the car as I drive through a long string of tunnels with limited signal[112]. It's still late enough (or early enough) that only a few vehicles are on this main artery between Oslo and Bergen and for once there is no rain, fog, ice, or snow to worry about. Still, I must pay attention to the random crossings of wild animals and ensure I don't speed, as speeding machines are frequent.

It's another good moment for reflection and evaluation of how I'm doing and what I should do (or stop doing) to be a better person. And when Whitney Houston's "One Moment in Time," suddenly plays inside the car, it could not be more appropriate.

At Vossevangen, one of Norway's top winter destinations, I turn southeast on National Road 13 toward the Hardanger Bridge and the small village of Odda, a township where Netflix's "Ragnarök" TV series was shot[113]. From there, I would reach Oslo in about six hours.

The infrastructure around the Hardanger Bridge, and the bridge itself, are quite impressive: roundabouts lit with electric-blue neon[114] are built inside the tunnels set before and after the longest suspension bridge in Norway and one of the longest in the world. Considering that the bridge is set between two galleries, the Hardanger Bridge is also the longest tunnel-to-tunnel suspension bridge in the world.

As I drive through, my navigation system resets our path to Oslo and suggests a shorter route following National Road 7. I check the time, and I realize that my adventure in Helle has used up most of the time I had initially gained by starting my journey earlier (thanks to the unsolicited outdoor "love cry" wake-up jingle in Bergen).

The new route could allow me to arrive in Lillestrøm on time and to stop by a few landmarks to take a couple of pictures. I also recall that during one of our meals, Øyvind had praised the beauty of the landscape I would pass through the same itinerary. Looking forward to seeing my friends (and trying to find a way to repair my broken relationship with my navigation system), at the roundabout drilled inside Butunnelen[115] I take the exit for National Road 7. Odda and my potential encounter with the Viking Gods' human incarnations[116] will have to wait for another time. My next destinations are now Eidfjord, a hot tourist location and a major cruise ship destination, the blue waters of lake Edfjordvatnet, the rushing force of the Bjoreio River, and the Vøringsfossen waterfalls—all stunning destinations, the beauty of which I completely miss as it's still too early for the first morning light.

It's up on the Hardangervidda mountain plateau that the sunrise surprises me, coloring the surrounding landscape with every possible shade and color of the visible light spectrum. Home to the Hardangerjøkulen, one of the largest glaciers in Norway, Hardangervidda is a mostly barren highland above the tree level, peppered with lakes, streams, and glaciers. The exposed rocks are covered with lichens and moss. Lit by the early morning light and pecked by mist and frost, they give a surreal sense of being on a different planet. But even on this desolate landscape, I find reassuring signs of advanced technology like a phone signal and a parking lot with multiple stations to charge electric vehicles[117].

My journey through the Hardangervidda plateau takes me past a series of captivating views. At the Skiftesjøen viewpoint I slow down and quietly take pictures of the lake and the glaciers in the distance, trying not to wake up a group of tourists sleeping inside their tents. A few miles later, I stop again by Halnefjorden, which is not really a fjord but a massive lake (the largest on the plateau) with its own port and ferry!

Suddenly I enter Viken County, which also includes Lillestrøm, my lunchtime destination, and home to most of my Norwegian friends. But I am not yet ready to be done with my journey. For the next 10 miles I stop at almost every single rest area or viewpoint to capture fragments of beauty that I'll always cherish. Once again, Øyvind was right: the drive through Hardangervidda is superb.

Whatever plans I had for the day, I ponder, would never have come close to this.

At a viewpoint in Haugastøl, starting point for hikers and bikers who, after a couple of days, will pass by Øyvind in Reinunga, I remove my binder from the passenger seat pack it for good inside my luggage.

At Haugastøl, the road starts winding down, and when I reach the tree line, the vegetation's red and yellow tones replace the icy cold greens and blue shades of Hardangervidda's lichens, snow, and ice. To my right, the deep blue waters of the conjoined lakes Sløddfjorden and Ustevatn[118] glimmers in the early morning light. At the end of Lake Ustevatn, I am surprised to find myself driving into the setting of some of the scenes in Joe Nesbø's fictional murder mystery Panserhjerte[119]. It's early morning, and I'm driving with the police detectives from cabin to cabin in the magic, golden hour of sunrise as light infuses the woods with red and golden tones. Now that I think about it, the setting would be more appropriate for a Tolkien-style, elven land than a thrilling investigation. I won't be participating in the final battle between Viking Gods and Giants at Odda, but at least I can imagine what my life would be as a Norwegian investigator.

Next, I reach Geilo, the winter capital of Norway. But as I live in Minnesota, and I get quite enough winter fun, I quickly move on, glad to be driving through the city in early fall when there is no snow on the road. The only thing that can stop me is the large number of speed-humps on the main street and the occasional farm truck carrying goods from farm to farm on the way to Nesbyen. At Gulsvik I stop by to see my friends at the CircleK gas station for a final refill of gas, chocolate, and warm rosinboller buns. As an additional benefit, the gas station offers a unique view of Lake Krøderen.

Lillestrøm, here I come!

- Hardangervidda -

14

Forgotten Friends and a Lost Wallet

Lillestrøm[120], the "Little part of the Strøm[121]," is no longer the quaint village I remembered. After days of driving through mostly remote landscapes, where I shared the road with farm vehicles, speeding trucks, and wild animals, I find myself in the midst of a town bursting with businesses, residential buildings and cars.

I reach the city with plenty of time to drive around looking for old, familiar landmarks. When I stop by a grocery store, once again I'm struck by the realization of how Norway has changed but has also kept many of its unique features. Having spent more than two decades in the United States, I got used to extreme excess and waste. Do you need a coffee? I'll give you dozens of choices and multiple sizes—never mind the fact that most of it is going to be thrown away at the end of the day. Cereals? I'll give you walls of shelves filled with all the sugar you may dream of. Paper bags? Be my guest: all the shapes, colors, and sizes.

But things are different in Norway. Stores are designed mostly to allow you to buy what you need, not necessarily what you want. Norway has very strict environmental policies. The country has voluntarily committed to reducing food waste[122] by 50% by 2030. Companies producing plastic are taxed unless most of the plastic is recycled, and waste is managed carefully. In Oslo, for instance, each household separates waste into color-coded bags: white, blue, and green. Food waste, collected in green bags, is used as fertilizer, or delivered to plants which produce biogas used to power public buses. This strategy gives citizens a concrete and visual understanding of how much food they are wasting.

Plastics, instead, are collected in blue bags and recycled. Any remaining residual waste is stored in white plastic bags that are incinerated for energy recovery.

In my quest to be as *in-the-moment-but-still-planning-the-basics as possible*, I had purchased a few gifts for my friends, but I neglected to bring with me paper bags and wrapping paper. As my luggage space was already limited and assuming that I could easily find the items in any grocery store like in the United States, what was the point of flying paper all the way across the Atlantic, right?

Wrong. I can't find any wrapping paper in the stores, and the only paper bags I can find are the grocery bags—something that we take for granted as a freebie in the U.S., but not so in Norway, where each bag has a price! In addition to that, Norway has very strict policies around alcohol, which can be purchased only in few wine monopoly stores. My European brain was set on Italian standards, and I was expecting to be able to buy a nice bottle of wine at any grocery store. As alcohol consumption was not an option for a solo driver like me, the idea of stopping be a Vinmonopoliet store to buy some delicious Italian Brunello or Barbaresco did come to me until it was too late. And with no cash or credit card, my options were extremely limited.

Despite my few difficulties, the big reunion moment arrives. I park my car, and while I wait for my friends, I quickly clean it up—just in case. The back seat is still full of clothes, now completely dry, and the front seat is strewn with electronics and camera gadgets all over the place. By the time my friend Turil finds me in the parking lot, my car is spotless and perfectly sanitized.

"You are early," says Turil, surprised. "You've changed."

"I know, too much time spent in Minnesota," I reply.

We both laugh at the thought that years ago, this naïve Italian was always the last one to show up.

"Before we forget," Turil opens her backpack. "The lost wallet."

"Thank you!" I exclaim, already feeling the energy that comes with my regained purchasing power empowerment.

"Try not to lose it again, will you?" says Turil.

"I'll try not to," I say, giggling.

"Follow me, my parents are waiting for us."

There was no need for Turil to show me where her parents' condo was. On my first trip to Norway, her father Bjørn, an engineer like me, had proudly showed me the design of a group of condos he and his best friends had designed. The goal was to finish the construction in time for their retirement so they could all live close and help each other as they aged. The building I walk toward is exactly as he had described it to me more than 20 years ago, down to the details—with one exception.

"The nurses' station is not needed yet," Bjørn answers with a wink when I ask why I can't find that specific part of the building. "Can we use your car to drive to the restaurant?"

"Of course," I reply. (Thank God and Odin I cleaned it up!)

With the easiness that is possible only among good friends, we spend lunchtime talking as if decades had not passed since our last time together. We talk about our families, our children (and their grandchildren), the job changes, and the trips to Italy.

"How are your renovation projects in Italy going? Are you still expanding?" I ask Bjørn, referring to his personal involvement in the reconstruction of a few buildings in an ancient Italian village.

"Sadly, I had to stop."

"I'm sorry. What happened?" I ask.

"Ah! The authorities!" exclaims Bjørn, making signs with his hands as only Italians can do.

I look at him, puzzled. "The Italian authorities?"

Turil laughs. "No, no. The Norwegian authorities."

Still confused, I turn to Bjørn.

Bjørn winks and nods toward his wife, Inger. "Norwegian authorities."

Inger nods firmly and we all laugh the loud Italian way. Completely oblivious to the fact that Scandinavian etiquette requires conversations to be carried with a calm, moderate tone[123].

The time comes to say goodbye. We all promise not to wait another couple of decades before seeing each other again.

Inger, the patient, committed, and supporting teacher who taught me how to read and talk in Norwegian, holds my hands. "If you wait too long, you may not find me next time."

"I promise." It's the only thing I'm able to reply without becoming emotional.

I leave Lillestrøm with mixed feelings of joy and sadness. "I promise," I say to myself as I drive to the airport to return my rental car.

"I promise," I echo to my mind as I lock my car for the last time.

"I promise," I mumble as the train takes me to Oslo, and the landscape sprints before my eyes.

- Friends (and Wallet), Here I Come! -

DAY 10

Stortinget (Norwegian Parliament)

15

Frogner Park

Like Lillestrøm, Oslo has changed greatly since my last visit. The population is almost three times what it used to be, and underdeveloped areas are now bursting with life. New businesses and restaurants have opened their doors, modern buildings have reshaped the look and feel of the city, and the traffic that used to overwhelm the downtown area is practically gone thanks to a web of subways, public transportation, and fast trains.

But in many aspects, Oslo is still the same lively, diverse, safe, and colorful city I left years ago. The charm of its history, the grandeur of its architecture, and the majesty of its waters and green parks are still there to be seen and enjoyed.

During my final visit to Oslo, one of the last things my younger version of me did was sit at the outdoor café of The Grand Hotel. It was a late summer afternoon, and Karl Johans Gate, Oslo's main street, was packed with tourists, residents, and members of the Parliament coming out of the Stortinget[124] to meet with their constituents. If there was a place where I wanted to be on my return to Oslo, it was The Grand Hotel. Thanks to my parents' sponsorship and my friend Leslie, who leads one of the best travel agencies in New York, my room has the best view I could possibly imagine. When I open the French doors of my balcony, I look out on Oslo's very heart. Even on a cloudy day, Karl Johans Gate is filled with people walking uphill to the Royal Palace to my right, or visiting retail stores, restaurants, and private residences on the opposite side, all the way to Oslo's Central Station. In front of me, by the gardens facing the Stortinget, demonstrators peacefully share their viewpoint with chants and speeches in the hope of capturing the attention of members of Parliament and the press. In the far distance, from the austere City Hall building, bells[125] mark the time at the sound of Imagine Dragons' "When I Ruled the World."

* * *

I LOOK FORWARD TO spending a day walking around a few of the capital's neighborhoods and to reconnecting with Margit, a friend I've not seen since my college years. Margit is not only a brilliant engineer, but also an expert in Norway's history and culture. Today, Margit is going to take me on a journey through time, from the foundation of old Christiania to the development of the latest modern districts. But first, I explore a few areas of "The Grand," walking through halls of historic paintings, furniture, crystal chandeliers, and enormous mirrors. I pass by Royal Suite, the Nobel Suite, and the Liberty style dining hall, the Palmen Restaurant[126], where I imagine people from all over the world gathering for receptions and events in honor of the many Nobel Price honorees[127] whom "The Grand" has been hosting since early 1900s.

I stop by the Grand Café, the original component of the hotel. It's a place that in the late 1800s was the bohemian hotspot of old Kristiania [128]. At the Grand Café, artists, explorers, and diplomats met to enjoy good food, share ideas, and change the world. During my breakfast time, I can't find any famous person, breakthrough inventor or innovative artist to talk to, but can certainly enjoy the food! Even though my system is still processing last night's largest kebab I've ever seen in my life[129], I find my way through an intricate and elaborate maze of delicious food creations I cannot resist.

My exploration of Oslo begins with some kind of a pilgrimage: a visit to the place I stopped before leaving the capital on my last trip to Norway, Vigeland Park and its monumental sculpture park of more than 200 granite, bronze, and iron masterpieces.

I leave The Grand and walk uphill to Karl Johans Gate. This section of the road, between the Stortinget and the Royal Palace, is wider than its eastern branch, narrower and older that in the past used to lead to the cathedral, the historic city center, and its battlements, while today it leads to Central Station.

I walk through a sea of red planters. To my right is the old University, and the silhouette of grandiose historical buildings now home to luxury hotels, restaurants, and music venues. To my left, a green belt of parks, statues, and fountains adorning the outdoor of the Stortinget and the National Theater. When Karl Johans Gate crosses Frederiks Gate, I enter Slottsparken and the boulevard leading to the Royal Palace. The open gravel path and the vast, green gardens on both sides of the boulevard add majesty to the sole standing residence of the royal family.

Slottsparken[130], the "Palace Park," encircles the Royal Palace on all sides and was designed at the same time the palace was built. The gardens are a collection of manicured green areas beautified by statues, small bridges, and ponds connected by a stream, all open to the public year-round except for the Queen's Garden which is closed in winter. Some of the park's features have been part of Oslo's history since the early 1800s. The ice of Ice One pond, for instance, used to provide ice for the Palace's cellars and some of Oslo's breweries.

Behind the Royal Gardens is the Uranienborg neighborhood, named after the Uranienborg observatory built in the 1500s on the island of Hven, currently part of Denmark[131].

Once a farmland with an exceptional view, nowadays Uranienborg hosts many historical residences from the late 1800s built for Oslo's wealthy merchants and entrepreneurs. Still today, the names of the buildings carry on the memory of the original owners like Villa Parafina[132], currently part of the Prime Minister's residence, built for Fredrik Sundt, first importer of petroleum, or Marmorgården, a label recalling the original farms and vegetable gardens that used to provide nourishment for the city. Other historical buildings serve as government offices, foreign embassies, or cultural offices, such as the villa designed by the Swedish architect Anselm Liljeström, which now houses the Italian Cultural Center.

There is no *straight* way to take me from the Royal Palace to Frogner Park as the street plan of Uranienborg evolved following the original network of paths between one farm and another. Still, I clearly remember how to get from one landmark to the other and at Riddervolds Plass, I continue walking on Briskebyveien, a street completed in the late 1930s that ends in Langaardsløkken[133] Park, what is left of Mads Ellef Langaard's loop property[134].

Briskebyveien offers a glimpse of how this part of Oslo transformed from the eastern border of a small village to today's modern and wealthy district. This is the place where Swiss-style wooden homes coexist with the early 1900s Neoclassic building hosting the Uranienborg Elementary and Middle schools.

At the crossing of Briskebyveien with Schives Gate stands one of the last 45 electric descend towers left in Oslo. Some of them are very decorative, others more austere. The purpose of this fascinating architectural[135] infrastructure, was to enable the maintenance personnel to climb down a ladder and access the electrical transformation stations set underground. The descend towers also provided necessary ventilation for the workers by allowing air to flow in and out of the underground maintenance tunnels.

Today, their functional use is obsolete, as they do not provide enough space to guarantee a safe access/escape, but still, they remain charming relics of a not-too-distant past[136].

The smell of food catches my attention. It's wet and a bit breezy, and I feel the need for some hot coffee. Just a few steps from the descend tower is Amaldus Nielsens plass, a park hosting the oldest flea market in Oslo, Vestkanttorget and, as the locals say, the best waffles in town—which of course I must try!

I'm fond of flea markets, as they give a glimpse of local history and culture. Flea markets are places where people of all ages and social strata meet, exchange ideas, and open themselves to the vulnerability of sharing, by negotiating a price, reasons why they like (or dislike) a specific item—and conversely, why sellers believe their merchandise deserves to be valued in a certain way. I stop by a few vendors to understand how items originated in various regions of the world may have made it all the way to Oslo, like the Polish painting of a Madonna. Sometimes the stories I hear are elaborate enough to deserve their own books. Luckily, I stroll around the flea market alone. Had I had my husband with me, I would have needed extra luggage to get back home, as he would have probably purchased many of the items on sale.

Hot coffee and engaging conversations in both English and my broken Norwegian are a great recipe to warm up both the body and spirit. But I'm also starting to have mixed feelings of excitement and uneasiness as I realize that I'm just a few blocks away from a place that is very important to me. It's as if my entire ten-day drive across Norway was just a physical and emotional journey leading me to my final milestone.

* * *

FROGNER PARK IS THE LARGEST PARK IN OSLO at 45 hectares (more than 110 acres). Its grandiose spread hosts green areas, ponds, museums, and historical buildings. Even though more than a million visitors cross its gates every year, it's very easy to find a section of the park that's still quiet and protected from the loud (and sometimes microphone-augmented) sounds of tourist guides, and the persistent cries of visitors asking for help with taking the perfect picture shot. If anything, today's persistent rain reduces the number of visitors to the park and increases the speed at which each tourist group moves from one section of the park to another.

Frogner Park is the world's largest sculpture park of works by a single artist—the "Vigeland installation[137]," a collection of bridges, fountains, wrought iron gates and more than 200 bronze, cast-iron, and marble statues. To many, it has the overwhelming feeling of being at an all-you-can-eat buffet with too many choices to take and limited time available. For me, it feels like being at the center of a multi-sensory experience designed just for myself.

I cross the front gate to plunge into the scent of countless flowers and the largest collection of roses in Norway, and I slowly make my way to the Oslo Museum and Vigeland's bridge in a futile attempt to slow down time. It's an ironic effort, in that one of the main themes of the entire Vigeland exhibition is time itself.

I enter the large opening leading to my appetizer, the Vigeland's bridge, a crossing point between a structured, systematic, and pattern-oriented world, represented by the manicured grounds behind me, and the cacophonous, unpredictable flow of human existence, which can be both beautiful and horrific. The bridge introduces me to a multidimensional storytelling of 52 scenes of men, women and children interacting with each other or simply sharing their feelings of happiness, triumph, love, loneliness, and anger with the visitors[138].

The rose garden at the end of the bridge acts as a transition feature that feels like a palate-cleansing sorbet served before the next course (or just an introduction to it): the Fountain. A group of six giants of different ages holds a large bowl representing the weight of life itself, from which water[139] rushes out, feeding a pool surrounded by tree-like sculptures representing the relationship of humans with nature. It's the beginning of October, and the fountain has been shut off, probably in preparation for the winter season. The only water feeding the fountain is the drizzling rain; but the lack of creation/destruction fluid doesn't diminish the expressiveness of the scene. If anything, the lack of water emphasizes each chiseled contour, expression or muscle preparing to face, with energy and strength, whatever life will deliver.

It's something that happens in real life as well; we are trained from an early age to quickly build our skills, master one branch of knowledge or another, and prepare for what will come. But by doing so, we neglect something else. We are so focused in preparing for the future that we fail to enjoy the present, to embrace what happens around us in that specific moment we experience at a given time—even when "enjoying time" just means losing ourselves in following a rational pattern to escape the maze tiled around the fountain.

The puzzling, but still regular and repetitive pattern shaped in black and white tiles reminds me of a typical life-journey. To each person traveling through life, totally immersed in a two-dimensional flow of choices, roadblocks and breakthroughs, the path may seem confusing, but the three-dimensional view from higher ground would show the simple, repetitive pattern of birth, development, growth, seniority, and death. For some, the pattern breaks earlier, their lives cut short.

The journey into Vigeland's world continues with another transition serving of artfully designed beds of flowers and staircases leading to the next course.

At the highest point of Frogner Park, protected by wrought-iron gates, stands the Monolith, a single-block granite sculpture of more than a hundred women and men of all ages and forms rising toward the sky in their struggling human strive to reach the unknown of divinity. Around the obelisk, 36 additional figures portray mundane events of men and women as they age. It's the circle of life that takes us all on slowly spinning, rhythmic dance sequences of steps that have their own distinct patterns but always share the same two stages of a beginning and an end.

It is here that I found myself almost three decades ago, sitting on the steps facing the final course of my sensory experience, the "Wheel of Life", a sculpture paired with harmonious and meticulously kept gardens leading to the exit gate. At that time, one cycle of my life had come to an end, and I had no idea what would come next.

Surrounded by marble-silent companions, I held in my hands a simple pendant I had on my plain golden chain: my last Norwegian coin. For the previous six years, Norway had been a magical place of discoveries, explorations, and strong feelings. As one stage of my life came to an end, I made myself the simple promise that I would hold on to that chain coin until I'd reached a new phase of my life; one that would be at least as meaningful as the previous one, if not more. Then I stood up and pledged to return to Norway, someway, somehow, someday. With no plans and no roadmap on how to get my life back on track, I walked back to the entrance of the park, one slow step after the other.

Years passed, and as one of the characters portrayed in Vigeland's storytelling, I walked through a maze of choices, roadblocks and gateways as passed from one stage of life to another: from one set of responsibilities and opportunities to another one.

Today, I sit once again on the same step of the Obelisk. I wear a different chain and pendant, but in the end, like all Vigeland's naked, timeless characters, I'm still the same person, although older and closer to the time I'll join the Obelisk's chaotic, uphill chase into the unknown. My stone-faced *buddies* have not changed at all since last time we shared the same foothold, but my life is different. I'm able to take time off from work responsibilities, family commitments and financial restrictions. My network of family and friends funded part of my excursion, and allowed me to be free of commitments, meal duties, and kids' homework or transportation. For ten days, I've been able to travel without prearranged schedules, set destinations, and settled times to eat, sleep or stop by a restroom.

Even the initial guilt of being away from family and obligations gradually melted away. By the time I reached Trondheim, after having slept on a boat, inside the car, or not at all, and after hours of driving and stopping just to take pictures or video of unforgettable places, I learned to *let go*. It's probably this feeling of being able to let go of responsibilities, duties, and concerns about what could go wrong, that allowed me to be so inattentive that I lost my wallet—and with it everything[140] that gave me a sense of security. (Gym membership card included.)

I've kept my promise of returning to Norway and I feel like the entire trip was the closing paragraph of my current chapter of life, with this specific moment being the final period. I'm ready to enter a new chapter of my own book, a new scene in my own circle of life.

- Frogner Park -

16

Rediscovering Downtown Oslo

I MET MARGIT WHILE STUDYING INDUSTRIAL ENGINEERING at the Politecnico di Torino in Turin, Italy. At that time, I was responsible for the organization of a training course held during the summer months for B.E.S.T. (Board of European Students in Technology) at the Politecnico di Torino in Turin, Italy. Margit was one of the participants. After college, I saw Margit a few times in Norway; then life took over and our connections were reduced to periodic LinkedIn check-ins on a few significant milestones such as birthdays or job changes.

"I just left my daughter to practice and I'm getting on the subway," Margit says. Her tone is as assertive and energetic as it used to be during our college years. "I've got lots of things I want to show you. Hope you are ready for a long walk. See you at the train station."

I've basically sat in my car for more than a week and a long walk is what I really need. "I can't wait!" I answer, as I take a few final pictures of Oslo's cathedral and one of those famous trolls set outside businesses and family homesteads all over Norway.

Oslo's Central Station is set in the very heart of the city and connects local and regional trains leading to Sweden and other, more distant European destinations. The main facility was built in the late 1980s, but the entire area was transformed in 2015 to become what is now an extensive complex of businesses, restaurants, and coffee shops surrounding the train station itself. Guarding the whole compound is a large bronze tiger[141] sculpture by Norwegian artist Elena Engelsen[142].

Our meeting place is the Espresso House, one of the coffee shops located inside the station. I wait for Margit the way a storyteller with all the time in world would—journaling, eating a pastry, and sipping espresso.

"Hi, I'm walking to the coffee shop," texts Margit. "You can't miss me. I'm carrying an orange umbrella."

The text wakes me up from my dreamy state of mind, and after carefully packing all my devices, I walk to the entrance of the coffee shop wondering if Margit and I will recognize each other after so many years.

I look to my right, scanning the crowd and searching for a colorful umbrella. It's rush hour. Shoulder-to-shoulder passengers of all ages, genders, ethnicity, and social statuses hurry to and from the train tracks. A hand arises from a dense cluster of people. It's Margit, waving. I recognize her long before I can get a glimpse of her umbrella. It's as if time has not passed at all. We are back in college catching up on our families, friends and key events that have marked our lives. "Now, it's time to get moving." My rational, I've-got-it-all planned Margit gets us both on track.

"Where do we start?" I smile. "You are the boss today."

"From the beginning."

"Of course, the old city." I nod.

"Not even close. We are going to the Opera House and the Munch Museum."

"Isn't that the most recently developed district in Oslo?" I ask, puzzled.

"Trust me."

And so, I follow my private tour guide through the streets of the Capital until we reach Operagata.

Bjørvika is the bay around which the old city of Oslo was built. The river Akerselva used to flow into the sea splitting the bay into two parts. In more recent times (and at the time of my last visit to Oslo), Bjørvika was an area characterized by heavy traffic congestion, as the land was shared by large industries, Oslo Station and its related network of train lines, and the European Highway 18, a critical infrastructure ending in St. Petersburg, Russia, via Sweden and Finland[143]. Today, the bay is very different from what it used to be. The highway has been moved underground, most of the heavy industries have been relocated, part of the river flows under the train station, and new developments, including housing, small businesses, the Oslo Opera House, and the Munch Museum have been built inside the bay itself.

Norway is a country famous for its free, open spaces, and the Oslo Opera House is no exception. Usually, I would think twice before walking on the rooftop of a building, but in Oslo, walking on top of the opera house's rooftop is not only allowed, but expected!

Managed by a government agency and built to host both the Norwegian National Opera and Ballet and the National Opera theater, the Oslo Opera House is the largest cultural building built in Norway since Trondheim's Nidaros Cathedral[144] was constructed in the early 1300s. The rooftop, made of white Italian Carrara marble, begins at sea level, and gradually slopes up at different angles, allowing the visitors to enjoy different views of the islands dotting the fjord, downtown Oslo, the surrounding mountains, and Bjørvika bay.

"What do you think?" asks Margit.

"I've seen a leaning tower[145]. But a leaning roof? This is a first," I say.

"Definitely. Now, look over there." Margit points to a small, yellow building on the opposite side of the bay. "It's one of the latest successful business additions, KOK Oslo Sauna, featuring dozens of courageous customers screaming with icy joy, as their just-out-of-the-blazing-hot-sauna bodies touch the refreshing waters of the ocean."

"Sounds like fun. I'll have to try it next time."

"I would suggest later in the year. For a full frozen-fjord experience," Margit says, giggling.

"Where do we go next?" I ask.

"MUNCH!"

"The painting?"

"No. The building." Margit points to a tower of recycled, perforated aluminum panels respectfully bowing toward downtown Oslo. The entire area surrounding the Oslo Opera House was under water when old Christiania was first built. The only thing left of the original shoreline is the name given to a few roads or parks. The Grønland[146] neighborhood, for instance, used to be the beach area east to the Aker River, while Grønland Street and Grønlandsleiret roughly follow the path of the old shoreline. But there is still one place that provides a glimpse of what old Oslo used to be in medieval times, Middelalderparken.

Opened in 2000, the Medieval Middelalderparken park was created to preserve and give access to the ruins of the churches of St. Clement and St. Mary, the former royal estate, and the reconstructed medieval shoreline[147]. The park is quite large, and if the weather is not collaborating, there is one place from which it can be enjoyed in a dry, warm, and comfortable environment: MUNCH, the Munch Museum.

The museum hosts various exhibitions, live performances, and workshops for people of any age, but if you make it to the 12th floor, you are up for a treat. Cocktail bar Kranen, set on the seaside glass façade of the building, offers an unparalleled view of Bjørvika Bay and Oslo; a sight that can be appreciated best from its sheltered terrace. On the opposite side of the building is Bistro Tolvte. From its windows, Margit shows me Middelalderparken and the ruins of Medieval Oslo.

"What happened to it?" I ask.

"It was built around 1000 A.D., and for about three hundred years it flourished. But then the Plague, Norway's economic and political downturn, and numerous fires reduced the city to a shadow of itself. The citizens tried to rebuild many times in the same place, but new fires started all the time until, in early 1600s, King Christian IV said, 'That is it. We're out of here. We're going to rebuild the city where I tell you.' And the old city was covered with dirt so that it could become farmland."

"Did he really say that?" I look at Margit, trying to figure out if she is joking or not.

"More or less," Margit says, smiling. "The new city, Christiania, was built on a grid stile around the king's Akershus fortress. To reduce the chances that fires would spread again, the new city had larger streets, and most buildings were made of bricks: tall walls protected it from enemy attacks."

"What happened then?"

I try to imagine hundreds of people driven away from a place their families have been living in for centuries to move to a new place. Did they do it voluntarily? Were they provided some *incentive* to move?

"Follow me." Margit walks toward the elevator and we get back to the ground floor. We leave the warmth and the dryness of the museum, but I'm now so intrigued by the idea of learning what happened to the citizens of Olso that I don't really mind.

We trace our steps back to the Oslo Opera House and then move forward onto Tollbugata that, as the name suggests, used to be the road (gata) leading to the customs (tolls) building for the city (by) of Christiania. "Tollbugata leads us to the heart of Kvadraturen, the city built under Christian IV after the fires of 1624. On your right, the old Stock Market building." With her right hand, Margit points to a charming yellow building, the baroque-style Treschowgården[148] built in 1710 for Gerhard Treschow, one of the largest shipowners of his time and an industrial pioneer of large-scale paper production. The building later hosted the Stock Exchange until 1823, the Oslo Cathedral School, Hotel Britannia, and finally it became part of Fredrick Olsen's office space for his Fred. Olsen & Co. shipping company.

"And about two hundred years later a new Stock Exchange building was erected." She turns to her left, and waves to a more classic, Palladian-style structure surrounded by Grønningen, the first public park in Oslo. Guarding the entrance of the "new" building of the Stock Exchange[149], a statue of Mercury, the Roman God of trade.

"I guess the employees didn't have to relocate far away," I remark as I look at the peculiarities of buildings that have shaped the economy and the growth of the entire country.

This section of the city was still part of Bjørvika Bay at the time Christiania was built. As the new city expanded, the bay was gradually filled, and the king allowed the owners of the new land to build as long as they paid for the expenses necessary to fill the bay.

"Ready for more?" asks Margit, her orange umbrella pointing straight in front of us.

"Of course, what's next?"

* * *

WE WALK THROUGH THE STREETS OF RENAISSANCE-ERA CHRISTIANIA. The city was structured according to the Greek Roman pattern of straight streets crossing each other at 90-degree angles, thus shaping square or rectangular plots of lands. Each plot (or "quarter," from the Latin word meaning "block") surrounded by four streets, took the Norwegian name of "kvartal," and thus the name Kvadraturen for the overall city plan.

We pass by the French patisserie, Pascal, open in the same location since the late 1800s, the old military school and post office buildings. We turn left on Kongens gate, a street that still leads to the fortress of Akershus and hosts the Department of Fisheries, so critical to Norwegian economy and growth[110]. Margit finally stops in front of Garmanngården, one of the oldest buildings in town, built in early 1600s.

"This building functioned as Town Hall, courthouse, even theater and events space from early 1700s until late 1800s. It was really the heart of the city," Explains Margit.

"A place where people met, exchanged ideas, and shaped the future for Oslo and the country itself," I comment.

"Exactly."

"But what about the king?"

Margit laughs. "Follow me. We are almost there." She walks a few yards west and points to a fountain shaped like a gigantic hand pointing to a specific point on the ground.

"Is that..." I start.

"Her skal byen ligge! The new town will be built here!" Margit proclaims, pointing to the ground.

"No chance of human error, I guess!" The giant shape of a hand pointing to a specific point in the ground marks the exact spot where the king declared the new city to be built.

"What would you like to see now?" asks Margit.

"I'm quite hungry. What about a traditional Norwegian meal, eating shrimps at the docks by Akershus?"

Margit looks at me, baffled. "You've really been gone for a long time."

"Why?"

"Come with me." Margit points her orange umbrella toward Rådhusgata, the street leading to Oslo's City Hall. Margit's family has roots tied to the Tromsø area. As we walk toward the fortress of Akershus, we talk about how life in Norway has changed since the early 1900s. "If you think about it," starts Margit. "When my grandmother was a child, not too long ago, families in the north of the country still had limited travel options to the south during winter, and most communications and transfers of goods were managed through sea routes."

Margit pauses for a moment. If I know her well, she is making some mathematical calculations. "Actually, now that I think about it, you would have never been able to drive all over the country in ten days like you just did. It would have taken you weeks," she says, confirming my initial thoughts. She has not changed. Her brain is still a human computer.

"And can you imagine traveling to Norway from the United States?" I add, and we both laugh, thinking how different our lives would have been had we been born just a hundred years earlier. My laugh stops as soon as we reach Akershusstranda, the street that forms a ring around the fortress. The road system that congested this part of Oslo during my last visit to Norway has been moved underground, and the entire area surrounding the City Hall and the Akershus fortress is now a pedestrian heaven. Sadly, with the development of more commercial and touristy infrastructure, gone are also the old piers where anglers used to dock and sell fresh fish. And gone is my hope for a bucket of fresh shrimp.

I turn to Margit. "Please tell me that you still have restaurants serving Norwegian food in Oslo."

"Of course, we do. But maybe not as many as we used to." Margit looks around, pondering a few options. "Italian restaurants, however, we have plenty! Follow me. There is a place I want to show you."

Once again, I follow her orange umbrella as we pass by the City Hall and the Nobel Peace Center. We stroll on Aker Brygge, a neighborhood that has been among the most popular in town since I was in my early twenties. On a normal day, this waterfront development of shops, offices, residential buildings, public areas, entertainment facilities and docks for small boats would be packed with people. But today, maybe because of the weather, Aker Brygge is peaceful and quiet, except for a few seagulls' squawks and the wild tantrum of a nearby child, which reminds me of my "fun" early days of parenthood.

Margit stops in front of a restaurant. "Here is Rorbua, my preferred Norwegian restaurant. It's small but the food is exquisite."

I enter the restaurant with the feeling of having been there before. A few months later, during one of my trips to my parents' home in Italy, I would find an old safekeeping containing notes and small items I had collected during my early trips to Norway[111]. I guess a few things did not change at all.

Entering Rorbua is like stepping into a vintage fisherman's canteen by a small village on the northern seashore. Tables and chairs are made of barrels. Nets, fish traps, furs, ropes, lamps created by placing a light inside the skin of a dried fish, and all kinds of sailing gear decorate the interior to give the feeling of eating inside a ship or a fisherman's cabin. The menu itself is journey into Norway's diverse cultural and gastronomic heritage. Boknafisk from the northern regions, Viltgryte, *Wild Stew*, with moose and reindeer meats from the woods that cover the land, and the delicious Skagenrøre shrimp and crayfish on egg, mayonnaise and dill crostini.

When the time comes to pick a desert, Margit points to a very special one, Tilslørte Lofotpiker, "Veiled Lofoten Girls."

"It's a variation of a very traditional Norwegian dessert, Tilslørte Bondepiker, or 'Veiled Peasant Girls.' Usually, it would be made with apples, but in the northern regions, including the Lofoten Islands, we use rhubarb, as it thrives up north," She explains.

"What kind of treats would your grandmother have when she was a little girl, up north?" I ask, trying to learn as much as possible about life and culture in Northern Norway, but also recognizing that our time together is coming to an end.

"Rhubarb crumble. I'll send you a recipe."

Our meal arrives and my taste buds scream with joy at the taste of my Torsk dish of cod with vegetables and potatoes in a sauce of butter and lemon. I savor each bite of it as I treasure each moment with Margit, until the time for the check comes and Margit must go back to her family. We promise each other to stay in touch.

"Try not to wait for three decades to come back to Norway. Ah! Look up to the sky, tonight. We may be able to see the Northern Lights all the way south to Oslo."

"I hope so. I've tried to see them for more than a week with no luck. And maybe next time I'll bring the family with me," I reply.

"You may want to skim down your plans then," Margit says. "Your journey across Norway may be too much for them."

I walk back to *The Grand*, passing a few landmarks once again. The Royal Palace, the National Theater, the Stortinget, even Karl Johans Gate are almost empty of people in these wet, late afternoon hours, which allows me to really enjoy my last few moments in Oslo. I cannot think of any other place for my last dinner than the historic Palmen at the Grand Hotel, a place where thinkers from all over the world met, exchanged ideas, and dined together as the northern lights shone above them.

- Oslo -

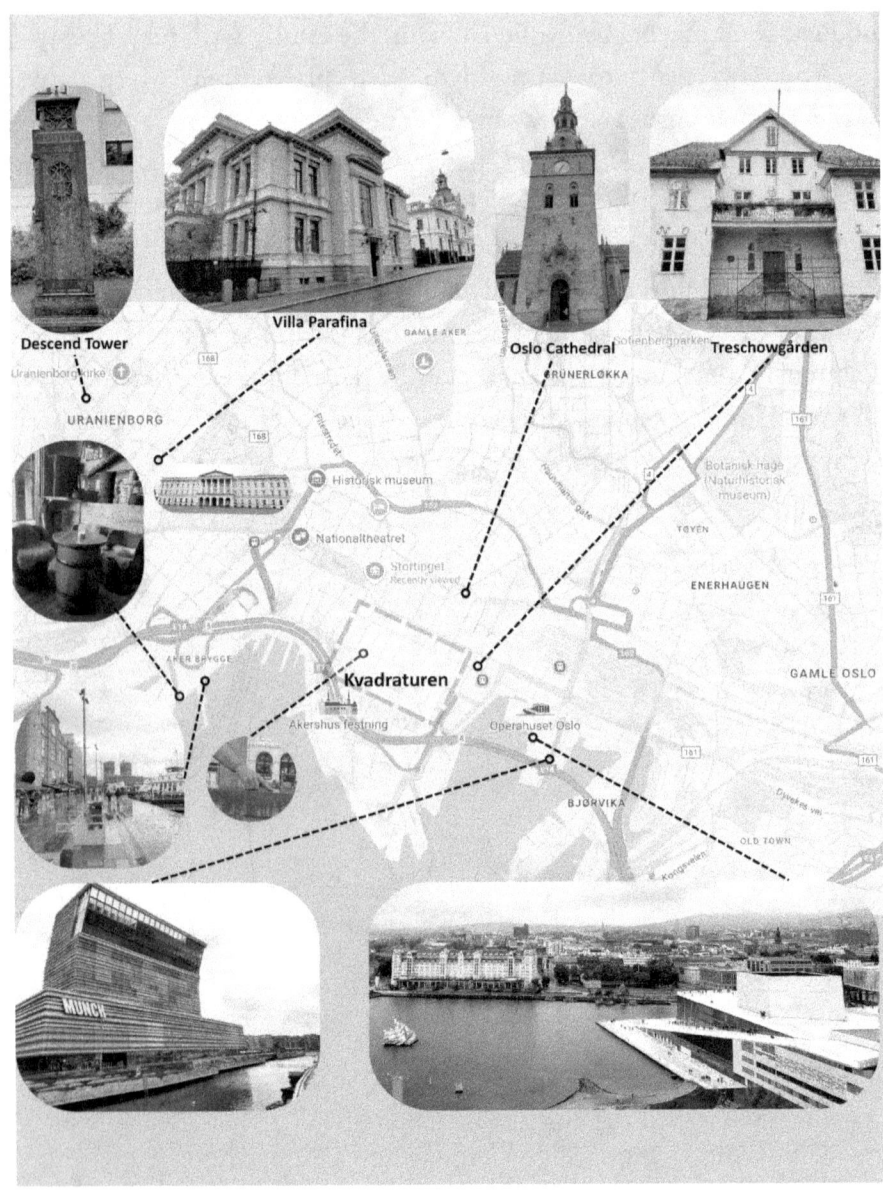

FULL CIRCLE

Street Art, Mural, Underground Parking Lot, Tromsø

Sculpture, Vigeland Park, Frogner Park, Oslo

17

A Journey Ends, a New One Begins

Thanks to the good people of Oslo, I wake up at 2:00 a.m. with tambourines and chants; no wake-up call is needed. Outside, in Magræssaparken, the green space outside the Stortinget, it's party time. I would love to join the fun, but my family is waiting for me. One hour later, I'm on my way to the airport, my taxi driving on the E6, the same thoroughfare that led me all the way to Northern Norway. I've come full circle. A few days ago, I left Oslo's airport to drive up north all the way to Tromsø. From there, I slowly found my way back.

I open my backpack and take out my binder. I had it all planned: a comprehensive itinerary including destinations, travel times, restaurants, and rest stops. As the expressway's high-mast light poles parade outside my cab window, I think of all the places I have been in a journey that only lasted ten days, but that deeply transformed me.

The trip started quite badly. Cancellations, delays, bad weather and roadwork heavily impacted what I had planned to achieve. I felt as if I were piloting a boat and had completely lost control of it. Until I realized that not being in control was exactly what I wanted to begin with. I wanted to reignite my thirst for going with the flow of uncertainty and surely I did get what I asked for. By losing my wallet, as the journey progressed, I had to learn to control my apprehension about the unknown, to adapt to changing environments, to have patience, and most of all, ask for help.

My friends in Oslo and Trondheim, the benefactor who found my wallet and called my family in Italy, the Circle-K manager providing me with his own pen, or the one who ran outside to return my credit card, the employee of the Ferry to Bodø, my family in the U.S., the owner of the B&B, they all lent a helping hand to ensure I could get to through my journey.

I close the binder. I've only been able to visit about half of the destinations I had planned to stop by.

Was it worth it?

If anything, it was useful to provide a reference point, any time my family wanted to know where I was. On the bright side, my deviations—whether intentional or otherwise—led me to remarkable destinations previously unknown to me.

There is only a short dark spot on the expressway to Gardemoen. In the distance, I see a flicker, just a few brushes of color painting the dark northern sky. There they are, finally, the northern lights! They may be as faint as they can be, but there they are, *waving* goodbye to me as I leave the country.

In return, I wave as well.

See you soon.

EPILOGUE

On the plane to Minneapolis, I scan the thousands of pictures and hours of videos I've made as I snack on the stack of rosinboller buns and Lunsj bars I have stocked up on at the airport. I have taken many beautiful pictures, but the one I like the most is the one featuring me sitting outside the B&B in Reinunga, just a few minutes before my train back to Flåm. At that time, I had no credit cards or cash, and I had no idea how I would make it back to Oslo. But in the picture, I look happy, at peace with the world, and ready for anything life might bring next.

Acknowledgements

This book would not have been possible without the help of many family members and friends who supported my journey financially and emotionally. Even though I drove solo for 4,740 kilometers (about 3,000 miles), I was never *alone*. Both my families in Italy and the United States checked on me occasionally, and my Norwegian friends did not hesitate to help me when I got in trouble. Even the gear I wore, the rental car I drove, and the lodging (e.g. hotel rooms, boat seats, train benches, and car back seat) I settled in, reminded me, all through the journey, of the love of everyone who sponsored my trip.

Special thanks to all my *guardian angels* who have helped me through the journey: Bardufoss Circle K manager for giving me his own pen to write my notes; Nammskogan Circle K manager for chasing me to the parking lot to return my credit card; Torghatten employee for letting me board in Moskenes; Grand Hotel Bellevue (Åndalsnes) restaurant manager for showing me how to link my bank account to a mobile app and hotel manager for allowing William to pay for my room; Circle K managers in Åndalsnes, Aurlandsvangen, Bergen, and Gulsvik, for giving me the opportunity to pay with my mobile app. And to you, Alan M., my Trondheim angel who found my wallet, my heartfelt thank you.

My sincere gratitude to Ed Letsinger who diligently edited the first version of the manuscript and provided valuable constructive feedback. Thank you to Carla H., Bonnie O. and Monica W. for helping me refining my work. Barbara, Brendan, Brianna, Laska, Linda, Margaret thank you for your support during our monthly writers' support group meetings. To my friends Bjørn and Inger T., Turil R., Marit S. and Øyvind H., tusen takk. Jeg står deg i evig gjeld, og du vil alltid være i hjertet mitt. Turil, thank you and your daughter for helping me reconnect with my wallet!

And finally, my loving thanks to William, Christian, Valentina and Barkley for allowing me to take time off and for the love and support all through the realization of this work. Silvia, Guendalina, thank you for connecting me with Alan and for keeping me grounded! Cosimo, Vincy (my parents), thank you for feeding my creative mind with trips to ancient cities, tales of times long gone, and lots (and lots) of books!

Suggested Readings

- Gaarder, Jostein. Sophie's World. First published January 1, 1991.

- Greentree, David, (Author), Bujero, Ramiro (Illustrator).

- Narvik 1940: The Battle for Northern Norway. First published July 19, 2022.

- Heyerdahl, Thor. Kon-Tiki. First published January 1, 1948.

- Ibsen, Herik, Peer Gynt. First published November 14, 1867.

- Nesbø, Jo. The Snowman. First published August 19, 2007.

- Nesbø, Jo. Panserhjerte. First published January 1, 2009.

- Sandel, Cora. Alberta and Jacob. First published January 1, 1926.

- Sandel, Cora. Alberta and Freedom. First published January 1, 1931.

- Sandel, Cora. Alberta Alone. First published January 1, 1939.

- Sturluson, Snorri. Heimskringla: or, The lives of the Norse Kings. First published January 1, 1230.

- Undset, Sigrid. Kristin Lavransdatter. First published January 1, 1920.

Notes

1. Hilsen fra Daniele, "Greetings from Daniele," was the subject line of the emails I sent to my Norwegian friends to let them know that I would finally be back to Norway after almost three decades.
2. Having traveled abroad for years, I have learned that it's always better to have a redundant financial system. For this reason, I have three separate wallets. If something happens to one source of funding, I can make use of the other two. Losing my jacket with all the three of them inside, however, would not be a fun experience.
3. Approximately 2,486 miles.
4. Oslo is located in the Central European (CET) time zone, which is 7 hours ahead of Minneapolis (CST).
5. Mythological Norse goddess of night and dreams.
6. https://bergstadenshotel.no/ .
7. Success factors as detailed in Chapter II of my binder.
8. https://www.schiphol.nl/en/ .
9. https://avinor.no/flyplass/oslo/ .
10. https://pilegrimsleden.no/en/interest-points/raknehaugen .
11. https://innlandetfylke.no/ .
12. https://www.arkitektur.no/prosjekter/landskap/rasteplasser-strandlykkja/ .
13. https://skogmus.no/ .
14. https://www.visitnorway.com/things-to-do/outdoor-activities/wildlife-safaris/experience-moose/ .

15. Spark, or kicksleds (English), are transportation devices made of a wooden seat, a standing place at the back to "kick" on snow or ice, and metal runners underneath. The largest kicker of all is installed in Tynset's main square. For more information, visit https://www.visitnorway.com/things-to-do/outdoor-activities/kicksledding/ .
16. https://www.visitnorway.com/places-to-go/trondelag/ .
17. https://www.visitnorway.com/places-to-go/trondelag/roros/ .
18. https://trondelag.com/opplevelser/sakrisodden-plantefredningsomradesibirstjerna/
19. Late 19th Century American English Idiom, In the Loop, A Reference Guide to American English Idioms, https://www.iowacourts.gov/static/media/cms/In_the_Loop_A_Reference_Guide_to_Am_34A595424C1B1.pdf .
20. Hell, Norway, https://www.visitnorway.com/listings/hell-station/214792/ .
21. "Hell Bridge."
22. Ferryman of the Greek underworld, Charon's duty was to transport the souls of the deceased.
23. https://visithelgeland.com/en/the-okstindan-mountains-and-okstindbreenglacier/ .
24. https://polarsirkelsenteret.no/ .
25. Approximately 1.4 miles.
26. The original Norwegian saying is "Det finnes ikke dårlig vær, bare dårlig Klær."
27. E6, opened in 1937 and asphalted in 1972, was closed in winter until 1968. The railway line was built during WWII and opened in 1947.
28. Raisin rolls.
29. https://www.researchgate.net/publication/254289037_Population_characteristics_of_the_world's_northernmost_stocks_of_European_lobster_Homarus_gammarus_in_Tysfjord_and_Nordfolda_northern_Norway .

30. https://maritime-executive.com/article/one-of-norway-s-northernmostferry-routes-is-set-to-go-all-electric .
31. https://www.museumnord.no/en/about-us/ .
32. https://www.britannica.com/biography/Snorri-Sturluson .
33. https://www.gutenberg.org/files/598/598-h/598-h.htm .
34. During the naval Battle of Svolder (c. 1000 AD), Olaf Tryggvason was defeated by a larger fleet led by King Sweyn I of Denmark, Olaf Skötkonung of Sweden, and Eric the Norwegian, Earl of Lade, https://snl.no/Slaget_ved_Svolder .
35. King of Norway (995-c.1000), later referred as St. Olaf for his efforts in converting Norway to Christianity, https://snl.no/Olav_Tryggvason .
36. https://www.visitnarvik.com/locations-narvik-hitlers-first-defeat .
37. Norwegian army's main base and military training facility.
38. Royal Norwegian Air Force base.
39. https://nordnorge.com/en/?aktiviteter=climb-the-sherpa-steps-in-tromso .
40. Named after Hans Rudolf With, captain in the Troms Fylkes Dampskribsrederi shipping company.
41. Video game created in 1984.
42. Alberta and Jacob, Cora Sandel.
43. The hotel is named after the legendary Hans Rudolph With, captain of the Tromsø steamship, Troms Fylkes Dampskibsselskap (TFDS) shipping company. https://snl.no/Troms_Fylkes_Dampskibsselskap_ASA .
44. The city of Tromsø is located on the island of Tromsøya.
45. www.ishavskatedralen.no .
46. Norwegian for Northern Lights.
47. Visitnorway.com .
48. Also referred to as "Devil's Teeth."

49. One of the most popular candies in Norway.

50. Visit Nordnorge.com/en for more information on the northern regions of Troms og Finnmark and Norland.

51. Hinnøya island is the second largest island outside the Svalbard archipelago.

52. Although I first relocated from the United Kingdom to Cincinnati, Ohio, and then moved to Crescent Springs, Kentucky, it is in Minnesota that I've raised my two children spent most of my life in the United States.

53. To facilitate the eventual crossing of two cars driving opposite ways, side stop areas have been set up in strategic locations. This allows one car to stop while an oncoming car passes through.

54. Discovered only in 2002, Røstrevet, the Røst reef, covers an area of about 100 square miles. www.guinnessworldrecords.com.

55. I wish I could share my mother's secret recipe for her own version of the "Stoccafisso alla Messinese". But there are many reasons why I am not in a position to do so; one of them being that my mother has kept it a secret from me, as well!

56. Drying flakes, also called fish flakes, are wooden structures built to facilitate the drying process of food.

57. Turil, one of my Norwegian friends, had suggested I stop by Børsen Spiseri to try the Tørrfisk Royal prepared by her Michelin-rated chef friend.

58. The Ocean-facing beaches or the hill of Hoven on the northern side of the island offer incredible views.

59. The original name of the island was Lófót. When the entire archipelago acquired the designation of Lofoten Islands, Lófót was renamed Vestvågøya. For more information on the Lofoten Islands visit www.visitlofoten.com .

60. www.nasjonaleturistveger.no .

61. By the end of the trip, there would be five "guardian angels" I would have to thank for helping me get through my journey: the ferry attendant was the first one.
62. "Har du røyka sokka dine?" (Are you crazy?)
63. Flemish northern region of current Belgium.
64. "Norway has just opened the world's most beautiful public loo", telegraph. co.uk .
65. Brilliant design and perfect location do not come cheap although this $2 million dollar designer restroom is not just a very expensive picnic area, but also a memorial to pay tribute to the 42 sailors who died when their submarine "Uredd" hit an underwater mine during WWII.
66. VisitNorway.com .
67. Fauske's Løgavlen mountain is the largest marble quarry in Norway. Fauske's' marble has been exported all over the world and can be even found inside the United Nations Headquarters. http://SLN.no/Fauske .
68. Blodveien, the Blood Road, was built by prisoners during the German occupation of Norway (1942-1943). During its construction, more than 300 prisoners died of exhaustion, hanging or shot on the spot. The blood Cross, Blodkorseet, was first marked on a rock with the blood of one of the prisoners in 1943. Since then, it has been repainted regularly. https://nordlandsmuseet. no/krigenskulturminner/blodveien .
69. Moirana.com .
70. Maaeffie in Southern Sámi.
71. Italian: "Where are you at?"
72. Sicilian: "Still have a long way to go".

73. Italian fictional character, www.pinocchio.it/en/collodi-e-pinocchio .

74. Nordland and Troms og Finnmark, the two counties that make up the region of Nord-Norge, encompass about 35% of Norway's mainland.

75. I later found out that it was fully booked for my only evening in Tromsø. Next time.

76. The "Thing" was a collective gathering of people designed to provide residents of different counties with a place to discuss, negotiate and align on legal and social matters. In a sense, it was the first nugget of what is today's Norwegian parliament. The Frostating was the Thing that took place at Frosta and had jurisdiction over 12 different counties. Visitfrosta.com .

77. Mythical magical creature with three times the intelligence of a man. heimskringla.no/ .

78. Visittrondheim.no/en/ .

79. Trondheim was the Capital city of Norway until 12a7 AD, https://Trondheim.no .

80. Some of the improvements include plants, trees, benches, tables, and new paving stones with underground heaters to keep parts of the square ice and snow free all year around. https://visittrondheim.no/.

81. The 1681 Horneman Fire that destroyed most of the city center.

82. Wide streets with trees lining up on both sides. Karl Johans Gata in Oslo connecting the Royal Palace with the old city of Oslo.

83. www.Nidarosdomen.no .

84. pilegrimsleden.no/en/articles/nidarosdomen .

85. www.caminodesantiago.gal/en/inicio .

86. The region of Innlandet was created in 2020 with the merger of the counties of Oppland and Hedland.

87. www.fjordnorway.com/en/attractions/trollstigen .
88. www.Tindevegen.no .
89. www.pilegrimsleden.no .
90. www.nobelprize.org/prizes/literature/1928/undset/facts/ .
91. www.visitnorway.com/listings/national-tourist-route-sognefjellet/233714/ .
92. Turtagrø.no .
93. Fortuna was the Roman Goddess of good luck.
94. www.norwaytrains.com/flamsbana-train.html .
95. The role of the "Horse Police" was to ensure the horses were well taken care of.
96. Øyvind foraged the berries from bushes growing in the woods surrounding the hytta.
97. Kinder eggs with interior plastic shell cannot be imported to the United States.
98. "Until next time", Norwegian.
99. One of the most spectacular viewpoint platforms in Norway. Visitnorway.com .
100. www.theglobeandmail.com/life/travel/disneys-frozen-inspired-by-norwaysbeauty/ article15617632/ .
101. Visitnorway.com .
102. Simple, but delicious porridge made from sour cream (rømme), flour, sugar, milk, topped with butter sprinkled with cinnamon.
103. Salt-cured ribs.
104. Colorful and sometimes festooned three-wheeled carts, mostly Piaggio's APE brand. Thanks to their small size, the carts have been historically highly effective in supporting vendors in driving through the narrow Sicilian streets to sell merchandise and farm goods door-to-door. However, they are relatively slow when driving on larger avenues or highways.

105. www.lifeinnorway.net .
106. During its history, Bergen experienced many fires. Torgallmenningen square was originally built as a firebreak for the city and it's now its commercial heart.
107. Daughter of the giant Jotun and grandmother of Thor, Nótt is the goddess of night, sleep ad dreams.
108. Veafjorden, was featured in some of the scenes of "The Golden Compass."
109. Reminder to myself to visit Helle once again for a fishing trip with my friend Rick.
110. https://movies.disney.com/alice-in-wonderland-1951 .
111. A Valkyrie in Norse mythology.
112. Wireless connectivity is usually exceptionally good inside Norwegian tunnels except for galleries under repair work or set in a few remote locations.
113. In Ragnarök, the town is called "Edda."
114. The blue lights are supposed to wake up and alert the brain.
115. Butunnelen is the gallery that begins at the other end of the Hardanger bridge.
116. Ragnarok, TV series.
117. At time of writing (2023) about 80% of new cars sold in Norway are 100% battery-electric powered. The country is on track to achieve its climate goal of 100% electric car sales by 2025.
118. The build of a dam at Ustevatn induced the water level to rise up to causing the two lakes to merge together most of the times. In case of drought, however, or whenever Ustevatn's water level decreases, the two lakes separate once again.

119. Panserhjerte literally translates "Armored Hearth", but the English title actually reads "The Leopard" which is also the English title of "The Gattopardo", a Sicilian novel written by Tommasi di Lampedusa.
120. www.lillestrom.kommune.no .
121. Strøm means also "river."
122. Approximately 1.5 million tons of CO_2 equivalents, oneplanetnetwork.org .
123. Even calling for the staff is not needed. A simple eye contact will suffice.
124. Norwegian Parliament.
125. Oslo City Hall's carillon has 49 bells and is programmed to play music of all genres with an hourly schedule between 7:00 a.m. and midnight. Live performances are executed on Sunday afternoon during the summer season. For more information on schedule and tours, please visit: www.oslo.kommune.no.
126. When The Grand was first built, the area where it stands used to be "outside" the city itself, so guests had to use carriages to get "The Grand Café"', the original restaurant that made up the first building block of The Grand. The Palmen Restaurant used to be the stables that hosted the guests' carriages.
127. It is tradition, for the Nobel Peace Prize winners to receive praises standing outside the balcony of the Noble Prize Suite.
128. Ánslo, the original Viking trade post was destroyed by a fire in early 1600. The new city was built by King Christian IV nearby the Akershus fortress and named Christiania, in honor of the king. Renamed Kristiania in 1878, the city took the name of Oslo in 1925.
129. Because even though I'd finally regained my financial freedom, my last evening was spent just walking through the streets of a city bursting with life—and I even joined the street dancing party in honor of the Karl Johan Hotel.

130. www.royalcourt.no .
131. www.visithven.dk .
132. Parafiin, or petroleum wax, is derivate of petroleum.
133. A "Lokke" or "Urban Loop" was land leased to an individual for agricultural purposes in exchange of a "Loop" tax. Urban loops were separated from "Takmark", common lands that all citizens could use to raise crops.
134. Mr Langaard's brick home, owned by the Oslo municipality, is leased to the Norwegian Rheumatism Association.
135. Reference: Norsk Folkemuseum, www.digitalmuseum.no .
136. The last set of towers was designed and set in place in the 1940s.
137. www.Vigeland.museum.no .
138. Even children's tantrums have a place in Vigeland's universe.
139. Water as the universal symbol of fertility, creation, destruction and regeneration.
140. My passport was safely stored inside my jacket's inner pocket.
141. Oslo's nick name is "Tiger City."
142. https://www.brandstrup.no/artists/elena-engelsen .
143. Prior to Brexit, E18 used to connect Norway westward to Scotland, England and Northern Ireland. The infrastructure is still there, but it has lost the European naming convention.
144. www.operaen.no .
145. Reference to the Italian Tower of Pisa.
146. "Green Land."
147. Oslo.kommune.no .
148. www.digitalmuseum.no .
149. The Stock Exchange is considered Norway's first monumental building, https://www.historienbakhistorien.no/.
150. Norway controls some of the richest fishing grounds in the world.
151. I found a Rorbua's bill and a beer coaster saved in a box I had left in my parents' home in Sicily.

About the Author

Daniele Sebastiano Longo is the author of *Angels, Love, and Lost Souls: A Journey to Sicily*, and a Prize Winner for the 2025 SouthWest Writers Annual Contest. Avid collector of old books, Daniele has lived, worked, and traveled in more than 20 countries and has moved nine times within Europe and the United States. Daniele currently resides in Shorewood, Minnesota, with his family.

CONTACT US

www.gerardandsebastiantravels.com
gerardandsebastiantravels@gmail.com

www.ingramcontent.com/pod-product-compliance
Lightning Source LLC
Chambersburg PA
CBHW071239070526
44583CB00017B/2257